Dehydrator Cookbook

The Complete Homemade Guide to Dehydrate Meats, Fish, Grains, Fruits, and Vegetables with Safe Storage Techniques and Easy to Make Recipes Including Vegan Dehydrated Ingredients

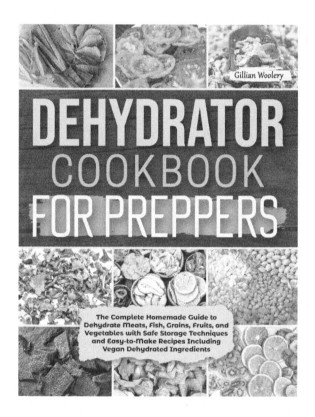

by Gillian Woolery

Copyright© 2023 - Gillian Woolery
All rights reserved.

The content contained within this book may not be reproduced, duplicated or transmitted without direct written permission from the author or the publisher.

Under no circumstances will any blame or legal responsibility be held against the publisher, or author, for any damages, reparation, or monetary loss due to the information contained within this book, either directly or indirectly.

This book is copyright protected. It is only for personal use. You cannot amend, distribute, sell, use, quote or paraphrase any part, or the content within this book, without the consent of the author or publisher.

By reading this document, the reader agrees that under no circumstances is the author responsible for any losses, direct or indirect, that are incurred as a result of the use of the information contained within this document, including, but not limited to, errors, omissions, or inaccuracies.

Please note the information contained within this document is for educational and entertainment purposes only. All effort has been executed to present accurate, up to date, reliable, complete information. No warranties of any kind are declared or implied. Readers acknowledge that the author is not engaged in the rendering of legal, financial, medical or professional advice. The content within this book has been derived from various sources. Please consult a licensed professional before attempting any techniques outlined in this book.

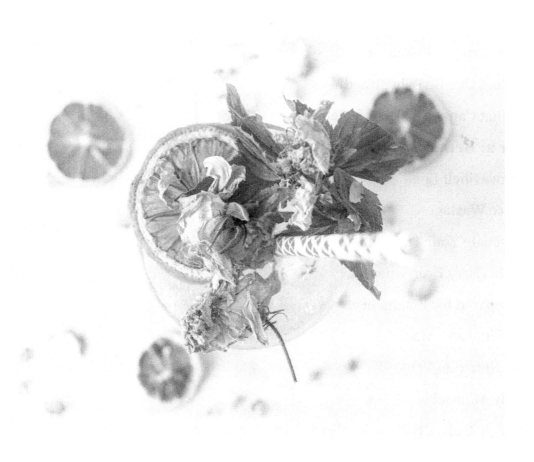

Table of Contents

Introduction	1
Chapter 1: Dehydrating Basics	**2**
What Exactly Is Dehydration of Foods?	2
Dehydrators	2
The Science Behind It	3
What Can Be Dehydrated?	3
What Cannot Be Dehydrated?	4
Chapter 2: Benefits of Dehydrating Food	**5**
Improve Shelf Life	5
Reduce Wastage	5
Rejuvenate Your TasteBuds	5
Easy to Carry Everywhere	5
Be Prepared for Emergencies	6
Save Time and Money	6
High Nutrition Value	6
Highly Affordable	6
Chapter 3: Dehydration Methods - In Depth	**8**
1. Sun Drying	8
2. Air Drying	8
3. Oven Drying	8
4. Solar Drying	9
5. Electric Dehydrators	9
Chapter 4: Storage and Tips for Dehydrated Foods	**11**
Tips to Dehydrate Foods Properly	11
Choose the right foods	11

Ensure proper moisture removal	11
Store in airtight containers or bags	11
Add sugar or salt	11
Be mindful of the temperature	11
Rotate your storage	11
Precautions While Storing Dried Foods	12
Check for signs of spoilage	12
Keep away from heat and moisture	12
Avoid cross-contamination	12
Discard any spoiled items	12
Storage Jars to Use for Dried Foods	12
Foods That Shouldn't Be Mixed	13

Chapter 5: Methods of Dehydration – Pros and Cons — 15

Pros and cons of air drying	15
Pros and cons of dehydrators	15
Pros and cons of freeze-drying	16
Pros and cons of solar dehydration	16
Check Readiness for Storage and Usage	16
Bring Back your Food's Life Through Rehydration	17
Advantages of rehydration	17
Disadvantages of rehydration	17

Chapter 6: Meat, Fish, & Jerkies Recipes(64) — 19

Western BBQ Jerky	19
Hamburger Beef Jerky Recipe	19
Herbs and Garlic beef jerky	20
Maple and Dijon jerky	20
Dehydrated Chicken	21
BBQ Mango Meat; Jerky Mango	21

BBQ Jerky Strips	22
Beef Jerky with Worcestershire Sauce	22
Beef Jerky with orange	23
Pastrami Jerky	23

Chapter 7: Nuts, Seeds, & Grains(39) — 51

Dried Beans	51
Texas Chili Peanuts	51
Maple Chipotle Candied Walnuts	52
Fruit trail Mix Recipe	52
Cacao dehydrated almonds	53
Maple Spiced Pecan	53
Dehydrated Peanuts	54
Dehydrated Chai Macadamias	54
Asian Inspired Nuts	55
Basic Soaked nuts	55

Chapter 8: Fruits, Vegetables(47) — 71

Chocolate Banana Leather	71
Apple fig fruit leather	71
Dehydrated Chives	71
Strawberry spicy fruit leather	72
Fruit Leather	72
Candy slices of watermelon	73
Honey Peaches with bourbon	73
Raspberry rolls	74
Apple chips with cinnamon garnish	74
Candied Pumpkin	75

Dehydrating Steamed vegetables — 89

Dried Broccoli and Cauliflower	89

Carrot Sticks	89
Corn Dehydrating on the cob	90
Dehydrating green beans	91
Dehydrating Potatoes	91
Spicy Mango Fruit Leather	92
Blackberry Chile fruit leather	92
Black and Blueberry fruit leather	93
Grape Maple fruit leather	93
Dehydrating Sweet Pepper	94
Chapter 9: Vegan Dehydrated Recipes(55)	**95**
Dehydrating tofu	95
Dehydrated tofu chicken	95
Red lentil chili	96
Dried Thai green curry	97
Thai red curry	97
Eggfruit lemon curd	98
Dried Coconut bacon	98
Vegan and unstuffed peppers	99
Tomato bisque	99
Mango salsa couscous salad	100
Conclusion	**127**
Thank You	**128**
References	**129**

Introduction

Congratulations on taking the first step towards prepping and preserving your food through dehydration! Whether you're just getting started or you're an experienced dehydrator, this cookbook is the perfect guide for preppers. With its introduction to dehydration basics, recipes, and tips on rehydration and storage, you'll be able to create delicious dried foods that will last for months or even years while still keeping their flavor and nutrients intact.

So now it's time to get out there and dehydrate your food! With a little practice and patience, you'll be making delicious dried snacks and meals in no time. Remember to always keep safety in mind when prepping and preserving your food with dehydration. From selecting the right ingredients and equipment to rehydrating and storing properly, this cookbook has you covered.

It's time to get dehydrating and enjoy the fruits of your labor! Bon appetit!

Chapter 1: Dehydrating Basics

Are you looking to up your prepping game? If so, then a food dehydrator is an essential piece of equipment. With this handy appliance, you can easily make dried fruits, veggies, jerky, and other snacks. This cookbook will give you plenty of tips, tricks, and basic knowledge that you can use to create nutritious meals and snacks with your food dehydrator! In this little guide, we discuss the basics of dehydrating, share some tips and tricks, discuss the pros and cons of different dehydrators, and provide some delicious recipes to get you started. We hope this book gives you the confidence and knowledge to create wonderful meals for yourself, your family, and your friends.

This chapter will cover some basic information about food dehydration that you need to be aware of before getting started. We will discuss the uses of dehydration and the science behind it.

What Exactly Is Dehydration of Foods?

Dehydration is a food preservation method that has been used since ancient times. It is the process of removing water from fruits, vegetables, and other foods to extend their shelf life. By removing moisture, bacteria and microorganisms cannot survive and spoil the food.

Bonus Tip: While dehydrating fruits and vegetables, it is important to cut them into slices of similar thickness so they dehydrate evenly.

This method of preserving food was traditionally done by sun drying, but technological advances have allowed for the use of electric dehydrators. As per a study by WebMD (2022), dehydrated food is nutrient-dense and has a long shelf life. Dehydrating your food is an efficient and affordable way to preserve the food for longer.

Dehydrators

Dehydrators are ideal for food preppers because they can take perishable foods and turn them into long-term storage items. Dried fruits and vegetables can be used in various meals and snacks, while jerky can last for months without refrigeration. Dehydrators are also great for making trail mixes, granola bars, and other snacks. You can also use them to make dried herbs and spices to flavour your recipes (Henry, 2022).

The Science Behind It

When food is dehydrated, it needs to be heated at a specific temperature and airflow rate in order to remove moisture without destroying the nutrients or altering the flavor of the food. The hot air evaporates water molecules from the food, leaving only enough moisture to hold the food together. Dehydration also reduces the weight and bulk of the food, making it easier to transport and store. For instance, a quart of apple slices takes up a lot less space than a quart of apples. As per the National center for home food preservation (2014), dehydrated foods can be stored for up to one year if they are kept in airtight containers and stored at temperatures between 40 and 70°Fahrenheit.

Did you know: Dehydrated foods tend to be higher in calories due to the loss of water weight.

What Can Be Dehydrated?

Almost any kind of fruit or vegetable can be dried in a dehydrator. Other foods that can be dehydrated include meats, nuts, grains, herbs, and spices. You need to remember that some foods take longer to dehydrate than others. For example, apples will take just a few hours, while potatoes may take up to twelve hours. Other food items that can be dehydrated include herbs and spices, slices of bread and crackers, dairy products like yogurt or cheese, and beans, mushrooms, and jerky (Cancler, 2020).

What Cannot Be Dehydrated?

Some foods should not be dried in a dehydrator as they do not respond well to this preservation method. These foods include dairy, eggs, and certain types of seafood. It is also important to note that raw potatoes turn black when dried, so they must be cooked before being dried. Why can we not dehydrate such foods? Dairy products are high in fat and moisture, making them unsuitable for dehydration. Eggs also contain a lot of liquid, so they are unsuitable for drying. And certain types of seafood, like fish, contain proteins that will break down during the drying process, resulting in an unpleasant flavor and texture. According to research by the University of Missouri (2021), dehydration is not suitable for preserving foods like eggs and dairy products.

> **Bonus Tip**: Be sure to read your dehydrator's manual before beginning, to ensure you are using it properly. This will help prevent any mistakes and ensure the best results from your dehydrated food!

Dehydrating food is a great way to extend its shelf life without harsh chemicals or preservatives. With a little knowledge, you can create delicious meals from dehydrated foods with the help of a dehydrator cookbook for preppers!

> **Bonus Tip**: When dehydrating foods, it is important to ensure they are stored away from any moist or damp environments.

Chapter 2: Benefits of Dehydrating Food

Dehydrating food has many benefits, including improving the shelf life of food, reducing wastage, rejuvenating your taste buds, making it easy to carry anywhere, and being prepared for emergencies. Additionally, dehydrating food saves time and money while retaining its high nutritional value. Dehydrated foods are also highly affordable as they require minimal equipment and can be stored easily. Let us discuss these benefits one by one in detail.

Improve Shelf Life

Dehydrated foods have an extended shelf life compared to fresh, frozen, or canned foods. The dehydration process removes most of the water content, preventing food spoilage. This means you can store the food for much longer without worrying about it going bad (Boxell, 2021).

Reduce Wastage

By dehydrating your food, you can reduce wastage by not having to throw out food that has gone bad. By drying the food and storing it in airtight containers, you can considerably extend its shelf life, reducing wastage.

Rejuvenate Your TasteBuds

Dehydrating food also helps it retain its flavor and texture, making it taste even better than fresh. The intense flavors of dried food can be a great way to spice up your meals and rejuvenate your taste buds.

Easy to Carry Everywhere

Dehydrated foods are lightweight, which makes them easy to carry with you wherever you go. Whether it's a picnic, camping trip, or a hike, you can bring your favorite snacks without worrying about them going bad.

Be Prepared for Emergencies

No one knows when an emergency might arise, and it is always better to be prepared. Having dehydrated foods stored in airtight containers can help you have access to nutritious food during emergencies.

Save Time and Money

Dehydrated foods require minimal preparation time, so you can save time and money by not buying expensive ingredients or cooking complicated recipes.

High Nutrition Value

Dehydrating food helps preserve its nutritional value, as it retains most of the vitamins and minerals that would have been lost during cooking. The process also helps reduce fat content, making it a great choice for those looking to watch their calorie intake (Silva, 2022).

Dehydrating food offers a wide range of benefits, including:

- Improves the shelf life of food significantly.
- Reduces food wastage as you can store an excess of fresh produce for later consumption.
- Rejuvenates your taste buds by creating tasty snacks from dried fruits and vegetables.
- Makes food easy to carry everywhere as they are lightweight and require no refrigeration.
- Prepares you for emergencies as it is a great way to store food without the need of electricity or other resources.
- Saves time and money by eliminating the need to buy processed, expensive snacks.
- Retains high nutrition value as the food is dried in low temperatures, preserving its mineral content.
- Highly affordable as you only need a dehydrator and minimal equipment to preserve your food.

Highly Affordable

Dehydrating food is highly affordable compared to other methods of preserving food. You can buy a dehydrator for relatively little money, and it requires minimal preparation time, too. However, it is important to note that certain foods should not be dehydrated as they may lose their texture and flavor. Moreover, proteins tend to break down during dehydration, so it is important to consider this before beginning (Silva, 2022).

Dehydrating food has many benefits and can be a great way to preserve your favorite foods! With a little knowledge and preparation, you can create delicious meals with the help of your dehydrator cookbook for preppers (Boxell, 2021).

With all these benefits, it's no wonder dehydration has been such a popular method of food preservation for centuries! Whether you're looking to extend the life of your fresh produce or just want to explore a new way of cooking, dehydrating food is an excellent option. So get creative and start experimenting with your very own dehydrated delights!

Chapter 3: Dehydration Methods - In Depth

In this section, we will discuss some dehydration methods in detail. Let us take a closer look at each one and understand its benefits.

Bonus Tip: Be sure to check your food often, as the low temperature of the oven can make it difficult to tell when it is finished cooking.

1. Sun Drying

Sun drying is one of the oldest dehydration methods and involves exposing food to direct sunlight for several days or weeks. This method is very effective in areas with dry, sunny climates as it does not require electricity or other resources. Tomatoes are an example of a food that can be preserved through sun drying (Ahuja, 2020).

2. Air Drying

Air drying works by suspending food items from strings and exposing them to the air. This method is perfect for herbs and small fruits as it does not require much energy or preparation time. An example of this method is drying apple slices on a clothesline.

3. Oven Drying

Oven drying works by placing food items in an oven set at a low temperature (around 100–150°Fahrenheit). This method is great for meats, fish, and nuts that are too large for air drying. For example, you can place sliced turkey in the oven to create delicious jerky.

Bonus Tip: It's important to remember there are certain foods, such as vegetables and fruits with high water content, that should be blanched before dehydrating to prevent the growth of bacteria.

Things to keep in mind when drying food in the oven:

- It might shrink/change color.
- Foods need to be properly spaced for better drying results.
- It's important not to over-dry the food as it may become brittle and unappetizing.

4. Solar Drying

Solar drying is similar to sun drying but involves using a solar dehydrator, which is essentially a box with glass panels that traps the heat from the sun while allowing the food items to be exposed to the air. This method is best used in areas with consistent sunlight and warm temperatures, as it requires a lot of energy. An example of this method is drying herbs in a solar dehydrator.

Did you know: According to the National Center for Home Food Preservation, the optimal temperature for dehydrating food is between 125–135°F.

Foods that can be dehydrated through solar drying:

- Fruits
- Vegetables
- Meats

- Fish
- Herbs
- Nuts and seeds.

> **Bonus Tip**: Even though dehydrating food is a great way to extend the shelf life of your produce, it's always best to store the dried items in airtight containers or bags to keep them free from moisture and contaminants.

5. Electric Dehydrators

Electric dehydrators use electricity to generate heated air, which is then used to dry food items. This method is the most efficient and provides the best results, as it maintains a consistent temperature throughout the drying process. An example of this method is using a dehydrator to make fruit leather.

Foods that should be dehydrated through electric dehydrators:

- Fruits
- Vegetables
- Meats
- Fish
- Herbs
- Nuts and seeds

These dehydration methods have their strengths and weaknesses, so it is important to find the one that works best for you and your needs. You can combine different methods to create unique flavor combinations or get creative with fun snacks like dried fruit leathers or crunchy veg chips! With a little experimenting and creativity, you could be enjoying delicious dehydrated meals in no time.

Chapter 4: Storage and Tips for Dehydrated Foods

This chapter will discuss the best ways to store your dehydrated foods for maximum shelf life. We will also provide useful tips for ensuring your dried food stays fresh and delicious even after months of storage.

Dehydrating food is not only a great way to extend its shelf life but also a great way to save money. Storing dehydrated items properly can help them last for several months or even years. Here are some tips on how to store and preserve your dried snacks.

Tips to Dehydrate Foods Properly

Choose the right foods

Not all food items can be dehydrated successfully. Choose fruits, vegetables, and meats that are ripe and in season.

Ensure proper moisture removal

Ensure you remove as much moisture from your food as possible before storing it.

Store in airtight containers or bags

Choose containers or bags that are airtight to keep your dried food free from moisture and contaminants.

Add sugar or salt

You can add sugar or salt to help preserve the dried food items longer.

Be mindful of the temperature

Be sure to store your dehydrated snacks in a cool, dry place away from direct sunlight to ensure optimal shelf life.

Rotate your storage

To ensure your dried food items stay fresh, rotate them throughout the year.

With these tips in mind, you can be assured that your dehydrated food will last for months or even years! Have fun experimenting with different dehydration methods and enjoy all the delicious and nutritious treats you can create.

Precautions While Storing Dried Foods

There are some precautions to take when storing your dried food to ensure it remains safe and edible. Here are a few important things to keep in mind.

Check for signs of spoilage

As with any food item, it's important to regularly check your dried foods for signs of spoilage.

Keep away from heat and moisture

Keep your dehydrated snacks away from direct sunlight and excessive heat or moisture sources. This will help preserve them better and maintain their flavor and texture.

Avoid cross-contamination

Make sure to store your dried items separately from uncooked or raw foods to avoid cross-contamination.

Discard any spoiled items

If you find any items with signs of spoilage (such as mold, discoloration, or insects), discard them immediately.

With these precautions in mind, you can be sure your dried foods will stay fresh and delicious for a long time!

Storage Jars to Use for Dried Foods

Using the right kind of containers is key when storing your dehydrated snacks. Glass jars are a great option as they are airtight and will help keep the food safe from moisture, contaminants, and pests. Mason jars make for perfect storage options as they come in various sizes, making them ideal for anything from nuts and seeds to larger items like fruits and vegetables (National Center for Home Food Preservation | How Do I? Dry, n.d.).

You can also use plastic containers with airtight lids, as they are lightweight, easy to store, and usually come in colorful designs that make them look attractive on your kitchen shelves.

No matter what type of container you choose, just ensure it is airtight and can keep your dried snacks safe from moisture, pests, and contaminants. With the right containers in place, you will be able to store your delicious dehydrated treats for quite some time!

Bonus Tip: When dehydrating food, make sure to label the containers with dates and ingredients so you can easily keep track of what you have stored. This will help you know when your snacks are ready for consumption, or when they need to be replaced.

Different food items and their shelf life:

- Fruits and vegetables: Up to 1 year
- Nuts and seeds: Up to 2 years
- Meats: 6–8 months
- Herbs and spices: Up to 4 years

With the right storage methods, you can easily extend the shelf life of your dehydrated snacks.

Foods That Shouldn't Be Mixed

When it comes to dehydrating different food items, you should follow a few rules of thumb. For example, certain food items shouldn't be mixed together due to their moisture or oil content differences. This includes anything from nuts and seeds to fruits and vegetables. Here's a quick rundown of which foods you should keep separate:

Bonus Tip: To get the most out of your dehydrated snacks, make sure to store them in airtight containers away from direct sunlight and sources of heat or moisture. Also, rotate your storage regularly and check for signs of spoilage.

- Nuts and seeds
- Fruits and vegetables
- Meat and fish products
- Herbs and spices

Why should certain food items not be mixed together?

Mixing certain food items can be dangerous because of their moisture or oil content differences. For example, nuts and seeds have a high oil content that can easily cause oxidation when mixed with other foods, thus leading to spoilage. Additionally, when fruits and vegetables are dehydrated together, they can transfer their flavors or aromas to each other. Finally, meats and fish products should be kept separate due to their high protein content, which makes them more susceptible to bacteria growth. Thus, it is best to keep these food items stored separately in order to preserve the flavor and quality of your dehydrated snacks.

According to an article by better health, processing food items by different methods can also cause a loss of nutrients and vitamins (*Food Processing and Nutrition*, n.d.)So it is important to store different types of food separately for proper preservation as well as to prevent the loss of essential nutrients. It's always best to refer to recommended storage guidelines from experts before mixing any food items when dehydrating. By keeping items separated, you can prevent cross-contamination and ensure the flavor of each item stays true.

Dehydration is a great way to preserve food for longer periods. When done correctly, it can extend the shelf life of different foods by up to four years. A study called "Osmotic dehydration of fruits and vegetables: a review" found that dehydration, especially osmotic dehydration can reduce moisture content in certain food items, thus preventing the growth of bacteria and extending the shelf life (Yadav & Singh, 2012). Additionally, it can eliminate odors in certain foods, such as onions and garlic, by removing the water content that causes these smells. Finally, dehydration can be used to retain vital vitamins, minerals, and other nutrients in food items for longer.

Chapter 5: Methods of Dehydration – Pros and Cons

Dehydrating food has various benefits. However, different methods of dehydration can have their pros and cons. For example, using an oven or a dehydrator to dry food is one of the most common ways. However, this method works best for fruits and vegetables as it can easily remove excess moisture without affecting taste or texture. On the other hand, air drying is best for foods like herbs and spices because it preserves the flavor (Porter, 2019).

Pros and cons of air drying

Air drying is a great way to preserve the flavor and texture of food. While it is slower than other methods, it can be very effective in preserving the nutrient content of food items. Additionally, air drying requires minimal equipment, making it an economical choice for those on a budget. On the downside, however, air drying can take several days or even weeks, depending on the item being dried, and it is not recommended for items like meats or fish due to its slow drying time.

Pros and cons of dehydrators

Dehydrators are great for preserving food. They remove moisture from fruits, vegetables, meats, and other foods so that they can be stored for longer periods of time without spoiling or losing their nutritional value. They are a healthier alternative to traditional drying methods like smoking because there is no open flame involved and the temperature is controlled. Dehydrators are energy efficient, using about the same amount of electricity as a light bulb for each hour of use.

On the other hand, Dehydrators take up a lot of space, so unless you have a dedicated area for it, it can be difficult to find room for one in your kitchen. It takes a long time to dehydrate foods, sometimes up to 10 hours or more, depending on the type of food and how much moisture it contains. Dehydrators can be noisy due to the fan that circulates air around the food. The cost of purchasing a dehydrator and the supplies needed to use one can add up quickly.

Pros and cons of freeze-drying

Freeze-drying is an excellent way to preserve delicate food items, as it does not affect taste or texture. It also preserves more nutrients than other dehydration methods due to its low temperature and vacuum process. However, this method can be quite expensive and time-consuming, making it a less practical option for many people.

Pros and cons of solar dehydration

Solar dehydration is great for those looking for an affordable and natural way to preserve food. Furthermore, it doesn't require special equipment or power sources and can be done in various climates. On the downside, this method is incredibly slow and may take days or even weeks, depending on the item being dried. Furthermore, solar dehydration can be unreliable in climates with inconsistent temperatures or periods of cloud cover.

Overall, dehydration is an excellent way to extend the shelf life of food items. While each method has its pros and cons, it's important to consider the item being dehydrated before deciding which technique is best. Whether you choose solar, air or any other method for dehydrating your food, you can be assured your food life will be preserved and the flavor will remain fresh as ever

No matter which method you choose, it is important to understand the basics of dehydration and how each method works. This will help you determine the best method for your needs and produces the best results. Moreover, take precautions when dehydrating food, such as using separate trays or sheets to prevent cross-contamination. Finally, keep an eye on the moisture content of your food to ensure it is evenly dehydrated. With the right know-how and some patience, you'll be well on your way to mastering dehydration in no time! Happy drying!

Check Readiness for Storage and Usage

Once your food is dried, it's important to check its readiness for storage and usage. Start by ensuring the product has cooled down completely before packing and storing it. Then, perform a visual inspection to make sure there are no signs of spoilage or moisture pockets. Finally, if possible, smell and taste the item to ensure the flavor and texture are satisfactory. If you follow these steps, you can be confident that your dried food will remain safe and flavorful for future use!

Bring Back your Food's Life Through Rehydration

> **Bonus Tip**: To prevent mold growth and preserve the integrity of your dried food, you should store it in airtight containers or vacuum sealed bags. This will help to ensure the food remains fresh for longer periods of time. Additionally, storing dried foods in cool, dry places can also help extend their shelf life!

Rehydrating your dried food is a great way to bring back its original flavor and texture. To do this, simply soak the item in water for several hours before using it. This will help restore the moisture content lost during the dehydration process, resulting in a tastier end product! Be sure to check for signs of spoilage before rehydrating and consuming your food, as this can help to prevent food-borne illnesses.

Advantages of rehydration

Rehydrating your dried food has numerous advantages. Not only does it help to restore the original flavor and texture of the product, but it also allows you to store dried foods for longer periods without them going bad. This method also helps preserve more nutrients than other dehydration methods due to its low temperature and vacuum process. So not only is it convenient, but it can also be good for your health!

Disadvantages of rehydration

While rehydration is a great way to revive dried foods, it does come with some drawbacks. For example, rehydrated food may have a different flavor and texture than the original item due to the changes in moisture content. Additionally, this method can be quite time-consuming as it typically takes several hours for the item to absorb enough water to be usable. Finally, rehydrated food can be quite expensive due to the energy used to heat and vaporize the water.

Additionally, it can result in over-soaking your food if not done properly, which can affect the flavor and texture of the product. And lastly, this method requires the use of special equipment and vacuums, which may be an overburden for some users and may add additional cost to your budget.

Chapter 6: Meat, Fish, & Jerkies Recipes

Western BBQ Jerky

Ingredients

- Lean Meat; 1 lb.
- Garlic Powder; ½ tsp
- Dry mustard; 1 tsp
- Onion powder; 1 tsp
- Brown sugar; 3 tbs
- Salt
- Pepper; ¼ tsp
- Red wine vinegar; ½ cup
- Cayenne pepper; 1/3 tsp

Method

Take a bowl and mix all the seasonings into it and put it aside. Cut the meat into ¼-inch thick slices and pour the seasoning on it. coat the slices thoroughly and place them in a plastic bag and refrigerate overnight.

Shake off the excess seasoning and put the meat slices on the dehydrator and process them at 155 degrees for 6 hours.

Hamburger Beef Jerky Recipe

Ingredients

- Ketchup; ½ cup
- Lean ground beef; 5 lbs.
- Accent seasoning; 2 ¼ tsp
- Brown sugar; 3 tsp
- Crushed red pepper; ½ tsp
- Liquid smoke; ½ cup
- Non-ionized salt; 4 ½ tsp
- Worcestershire sauce; ½ cup
- Meat tenderizer; 2 ¼ tbs
- Garlic powder; ¾ tsp
- Pepper; ¾ tbs

Method

Take a bowl, and add the ingredients excluding ground beef, Worcestershire sauce, ketchup, and liquid smoke. Process the meat from the jerky gun and mix it with the other ingredients and dip them in the sauce mixture.

Put the jerky strips on the dehydrator tray and process them at 155 degrees for 4 to 8 hours.

Herbs and Garlic beef jerky

Ingredients

- *Lean ground beef; 1 lb.*
- *Garlic cloves; 6*
- *Oregano fresh; 1 tbs*
- *Salt*
- *Black pepper; ½ tsp*
- *Parsley; 1 cup chopped*
- *Onions; chopped; ½ cup*
- *Sage; chopped ½ cup*

Method

Process beef, onion, parsley, oregano, salt, pepper, sage, and garlic till it forms the paste. When done, process it from the jerky gun.

Place the strips on the baking sheet and process them for 7 to 8 hours at 155 degrees.

Maple and Dijon jerky

Ingredients

- *Pure maple syrup; 2 tbs*
- *Meat; 1lb.*
- *Grainy Dijon mustard*
- *Salt; ¼ tsp*

Method

Before cutting the meat slices, put them in the freezer to cut firm slices. Make sure the slices are not thicker than ¼ inch. Take a bowl and add maple syrup, mustard, and salt. Toss them to coat the meat strips properly, place them in a plastic bag and marinate it overnight.

Preheat oven to 300 degrees and bake them for 10 minutes for till the meat turns brown. Place them on the dehydrator tray with distance and process them at 155 degrees for 7 to 9 hours.

Dehydrated Chicken

Ingredients

- *Chicken breast; 5 lbs.*

Method

Marinate the chicken overnight with any recipe and pressure

cook it for 12 minutes. Cool it down and cut them into slices

in the grain direction.

Place the slices on the dehydrator tray and process them for 12 hours at 125 degrees.

Store them in an airtight container.

BBQ Mango Meat; Jerky Mango

This taste is **purely vegan** made with mango chunks or you can say mango jerky with rich spices. To make this,

Ingredients,

- *Mango, unripe; 1*
- *Chili powder/chipotle; ½ tsp*
- *Paprika, smoked; ½ tsp*
- *Cumin seed powder; ¼ tsp*
- *Salt & pepper; as taste*

Method,

Peel the mango and cut it into small cubes. Add them to a bowl and mix along with all the spices. Spread all the mango cubes on the dehydrator sheet and dehydrate it for around **1 to 2 hours** or till it becomes crispy at the temperature of **115 degrees F**.

This can be stored for around a week in a container at room temperature. It will take a maximum of 2 days to dry completely. ***If you want to speed up the process, cut the mangoes into long strips, it will dry them up fast.***

It can be a part of your vegan bbq by adding cherry tomatoes, onions, and other vegetables.

BBQ Jerky Strips

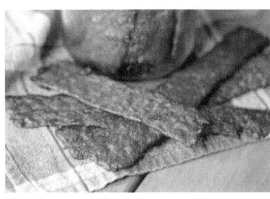

Ingredients

- *Ground beef; 2 ½ lbs.*
- *Garlic powder; ½ tsp*
- *Onion powder; ½ tsp*
- *Brown sugar; 1 ½ tbs*
- *Worcestershire sauce; ¼ cup*
- *Barbecue sauce, diluted with water; ½ cup*

Method

Mix ground beef with the ingredients in a bowl. Add bbq sauce, slightly diluted with water, and coat it with beef strips. Squeeze the beef strips into the jerky gun and place it on the dehydrator at 145 to 155 degrees F for 6 to 12 hours.

Beef Jerky with Worcestershire Sauce

Ingredients

- *Lean meat sliced; 2 lbs.*
- *Soy sauce; ¼ cup*
- *Hot sauce; 1 tsp*
- *Worcestershire Sauce; 1 tsp*
- *Onion powder; ¼ tsp*
- *Garlic powder; ¼ tsp*
- *Paprika; ¼ tsp*
- *Liquid smoke; 1 tsp*
- *Pepper; ¼ tsp*

Method

The meat strips must be cut into ¼ inch thick and coated with all the ingredients evenly. Let these marinated beef strips in the refrigerator overnight.

On the dehydrator, set the temperature to 145 to 155 degrees for 6 and 6 hours.

Beef Jerky with orange

Ingredients

- *Lean beef, fat trimmed; 3 lbs.*
- *Orange; 2 peeled, 1 zest*
- *Soy sauce; 3 tbs*
- *Rice vinegar; 3 tbs*
- *Sugar; 2 tbs*
- *Sesame oil; 3 tbs*
- *Toasted sesame oil; 1 ½ tbs*
- *Asian chili garlic paste; 1 tsp*
- *Fresh ginger, grated; 2 tbs*

Method

Take the blender and blend the seasoning in it, mix them well. Cut the beef into slices, ¼ inch thick strips and mix it with the beef, marinate it overnight in the refrigerator.

Next day, bring the beef out and let it come to normal room temperature, and place it on the dehydrator tray afterward in a single layer.

Turn on the dehydrator at 145 to 160 degrees F for 6 – 6 hours by flipping in between.

Pastrami Jerky

Ingredients

- *Lean beef; 3 lbs.*
- *Soy sauce; ½ cup*
- *Brown sugar; ¼ cup*
- *Worcestershire sauce; ½ cup*
- *Lemon juice; 1 tbs*
- *Mustard seeds; 1 tbsp*
- *Coriander seeds; 2 tbsp*
- *Cayenne pepper; ½ tsp*
- *Coarse pepper seeds; 2 tbsp*

Method

Cut the lean beef into slices of ¼ inch thick strips. Mix all the ingredients excluding all the seeds. Pour the mixture on the meat and let it sit overnight in the refrigerator.

When done, bring it to room temperature first and place it neatly on the dehydrator tray and sprinkle the seeds on it. let them dehydrate at 145 to 155 degrees for 6-6 hours.

Salmon Jerky with teriyaki sauce

Ingredients

- *Salmon, boneless; 1 ½ lb.*
- *Teriyaki sauce; ¼ cup*
- *Soy sauce; ¼ cup*
- *Maple syrup; 1 tbs*
- *Dijon mustard; 1 tsp*
- *Lime, squeezed; 1*
- *Black pepper; ½ tsp*

Method

Here is a tip, **before slicing the salmon, freeze it for almost 1 hour.** Take a bowl and mix all the seasonings, and whisk them well.

Dip the salmon slices in the mixture and let it soak for 3 hours. Shake off the excess liquid and put them on the dehydrator tray.

Dry salmon in your dehydrator, and place it at 155 degrees F for 10 to 12 hours.

Smoked Mexican Jerky

Ingredients

- *Beef, fat trimmed; 2 lbs.*
- *Soy sauce; ½ cup*
- *Fresh lime; 1 cup*
- *Mexican beer; 1 cup*
- *Chili powder; 1 tsp*
- *Chipotle peppers in adobo sauce; 1-2 can*

Method

Mix the ingredients in a bowl excluding the beef in a food processor and make it smooth. Pour the mixture onto the beef and marinate it for 6 hours in the refrigerator.

Bring it to room temperature and place the strips separately in a single layer on the dehydrator tray. Let it process for 6-6 hours at 145 to 160 degrees.

Turkey Jerky with Red chili flakes

Ingredients

- *Skinless and boneless Turkey; 2 lbs.*
- *Brown sugar; 3 tbs*
- *Chopped garlic; 2 tsp*
- *Red chili flakes; 2 tsp*
- *Soy sauce; ¾ cup*

Method

Before slicing the turkey, make sure it is frozen and then cut ¼ inch thick slices into strips. Mix the ingredients in a bowl and dip the strips into it so that they are coated and marinated.

Cover the marinated turkey with a cling and leave it overnight in the refrigerator. When 9one, place the slices on the dehydrator tray and let it dry at 155 degrees for 8 to 6 hours.

Harissa-flavored Beef Jerky

Ingredients

- *Lean beef, eye round; 3 lbs.*
- *Brown sugar; 1 tbs*
- *Salt*
- *Cumin; 1 tbs*
- *Smoked paprika; 1 tbs*
- *Coriander; 1 tbs*
- *Garlic powder; 1 tbs*
- *Onion powder; 2 tbs*
- *Cayenne pepper; ¼ tsp*
- *Chili powder; 1 tbs*

Method

Cut the eye-round beef into thick strips, not more than ¼ inch/. Mix the ingredients in a zip-lock bag, shake it well, and add the beef strips. Leave it in the refrigerator overnight.

Bring the beef strip to room temperature and place the strips on the dehydrator tray to dry at 145 to 155 degrees for 6 and 6 hours.

Sweet and Spicy beef Jerky

Ingredients

- *Venison or beef; 2 lbs.*
- *Sriracha sauce; 1 tsp.*
- *Soy sauce; 1 tsp*
- *Lemon juice; 1 tbs*
- *Minced garlic; 1 tbs*
- *Soy sauce; ½ cup*
- *Worcestershire sauce; ¼ cup*
- *Brown sugar; ½ cup*
- *Pineapple juice; ¼*
- *Black pepper; 1 tbs*

Method

Slice frozen meat or venison into ¼-inch thick pieces. Combine all of the ingredients, then coat the strips in the sauce, cover them, and put them in the fridge. Arrange slices of beef or venison on dehydrator trays and dry at 145 to 155 degrees, roughly six to six hours.

Worcestershire seasoned Beef Jerky

Ingredients

- *Lean beef; 2 lbs.*
- *Honey; 3 tbs*
- *Lemon juice; 1 tsp*
- *Red pepper flake; 1 tbs*
- *Teriyaki sauce; 1 cup*
- *Onion powder; 2 tsp*
- *Garlic powder; 2 tsp*
- *Ground ginger; 1 tsp*
- *Paprika; 1 tbs*
- *Worcestershire sauce; 1 cup*

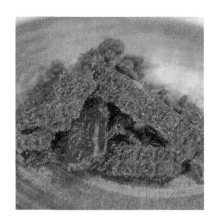

Method

Slice the strips into ¼-inch-thick pieces. Combine the ingredients, and marinate the meat in the mixture. Cover and place in the fridge for the night. Spread out the beef slices on the dehydrator trays and dry at 145 to 155 degrees for 6 to 8 hours.

Thai sweet chili jerky

Ingredients

- *Beef, fat trimmed, ¼ inch sliced; 2 lbs.*
- *Teriyaki sauce; 1 tbs*
- *Water; ½ cup*
- *Ground ginger; 1 tsp*
- *Sweet chili sauce; 1 cup*
- *Soy sauce; 1 tbs*
- *Worcestershire Sauce; 1 tbs*

Method

In a bowl, mix the ingredients for the marinade. Fill a zip-lock bag with meat, then add the marinade.

Let the beef sit with the marinated mixture overnight in the refrigerator. Arrange the meat in a single layer on the sheets of the dehydrator. For 6 to 8 hours, dehydrate at 155 degrees.

Hot and spicy Jerky with Boozy touch

Ingredients

- Lean steak; 2 lbs.
- Belgian beer dark; 16 ounces
- Cayenne pepper; ½ tsp
- Garlic cloves, minced; 2
- Seasoned salt; 2 tbs
- Teriyaki Sauce; ¼ cup
- Dark brown sugar; 2 tbs

Method

Take a bowl, and combine all the ingredients. Fill a zip-lock bag with meat, then add the mixture. Leave the meat in the refrigerator. Bring it to normal room temperature level.

Spread the meat out in a single layer on dehydrator sheets. Dehydrate for 6–8 hours at 160°F.

Asian Jerky

Ingredients

- *Lean beef; 1 lb.*
- *Pepper; ½ tsp*
- *Honey; 1 tsp*
- *Soy sauce; 4 tbs*
- *Worcestershire sauce; 4 tbs*
- *Toasted Sesame oil; 1 tsp*
- *Garlic; 3 cloves*
- *Soy sauce; 4 tbs*

Method

Cut the beef into strips, ¼ inch slice each. Blend the ingredients and coat every strip with it evenly, cover it, and put it in the refrigerator overnight.

Put the beef jerky on the dehydrator tray for 6—6 hours at 1415 to 155 degrees.

Beef Jerky with Garlic

Ingredients

- *Thinly sliced beef; 2 lbs.*
- *Soy sauce; ½ cup*
- *Worcestershire sauce; 3 tbs*
- *Can of coke; 1*
- *Garlic, crushed; 7 cloves*
- *Red hot sauce; 2 tsp*
- *Fresh lime juice; 1 tsp*
- *Ketchup; 2 tbs*

Method

Combine the ingredients and marinate in a large bowl. Place the meat in the zip-lock bag and pour the mixture. Leave it in the refrigerator for 4 to 8 hours.

Place them on the dehydrating tray as a single layer for 6 to 8 hours at 155 degrees F.

Marinated Jerky

Ingredients

- Sliced lean meat; 2 lbs.
- Smoked paprika; ½ tsp
- Liquid smoke; 2 tbs
- Sugar; ¼ cup
- Salt; 1 cup and 1 tbs
- Water; ½ gallon
- Black pepper; ½ tsp

Method

Cut the meat into ½ inch slices. Prepare the mixture will all the ingredients and soak the meat strips into it. put them on a dehydrator tray for 6-6 hours at 145 to 155 degrees F temperature.

Pork Jerky and chipotle sauce

Ingredients

- *Tomato paste; 1 tbs*
- *Chipotle sauce; 7 oz.*
- *Salt; 1 tsp*
- *Sugar; 1 tsp*
- *Pork, sliced; 1 lb.*

Method

Mix the tomato paste with other ingredients and place them all in the zip-lock bag. Refrigerate it for 12 hours. When done, place it on the dehydrator tray at 159 degrees temperature for 6 hours.

Remember to store that away from the sunlight.

Pork Jerky with Paprika

Ingredient

- Pork tenderloin, sliced; 1 lb.
- Salt and pepper
- Onion powder; 1 tsp
- Chili powder; 1 tsp
- Mustard, ground; 1 tsp
- Garlic powder; 1 tsp
- Ketchup; ½ cup
- Smoked paprika; 1 tsp

Method

Take a bowl and add ketchup, stir the onion, garlic, paprika, chili, mustard, etc. powder and mix them well. Place the pork in an airtight bag along with the mixture and refrigerate for 12 hours.

Place the meat on the dehydrator tray and dry it at 158 degrees for 6 hours.

Spiced Jerky Hamburger

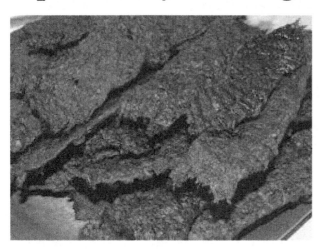

Ingredients

- Ground beef; 2 ½ lbs.
- Adobo seasoning; 1 tsp
- Garlic powder; ½ tsp
- Onion; ½ tsp
- Worcestershire sauce; ¼ cup
- Liquid smoke; ¼ cup
- Tomato sauce; ¼ cup
- Salt
- Meat tenderizer; 1 tbs
- Cayenne pepper; ½ tsp

Methods

Mix the ground beef with dry ingredients and combine the liquids. Make sure the beef strips are coated well with the mixture. Press the beef strips with the help of a jerky gun.

Let it process in a dehydrator for 6 to 12 hours at 145 to 155 degrees temperature.

Beef Bulgogi jerky

Ingredients

- *Beef round and sliced; 2 lbs.*
- *Brown sugar; 2tbs*
- *Soy sauce; 4 tbs*
- *Garlic powder; 1 tbs*
- *Sesame oil; 1 tbs*
- *Salt*

Method

Cut the beef slices to 5mm thick. Place the beef in the zip-lock or a plastic bag. Mix the other ingredients in the bowl and later add it to the plastic bag and refrigerate it for 12 hours.

When done, remove the excess marinade and place the beef on the dehydrator tray at 165 degrees and let it process for 6 hours.

Mustard Beef jerky with balsamic vinegar

Ingredients

- *Beef ground, sliced; 2 lbs.*
- *Dijon mustard; 1 tbs*
- *Garlic cloves; 2 crushed*
- *Salt*
- *Olive oil; 2 tbs*
- *Balsamic vinegar 1 cup*

Method

Take a plastic bag and add the beef. Combine the ingredients in a bowl and whisk them. Now pour the mixture into the beef bag. Leave it for 12 hours in the fridge, and drain the excess marinade.

Place the beef on the dehydrator tray and turn it on at 165 degrees for 6 hours, till it dries well.

Buffalo jerky

Ingredients

- *Beef, sliced; 2 lbs.*
- *Salt*
- *Buffalo sauce*

Method

Take a bowl, season the beef with salt, and add the buffalo sauce. Mix them well, cover them and leave them in the refrigerator for 15 hours.

Remove extra marinade, and place it on the dehydrator tray for 6 hours at 165 degrees.

BBQ beef jerky

Ingredient

- *Beef, round and sliced; 2 lbs.*
- *Red pepper flakes; 1 tsp*
- *Grated garlic; 4 cloves*
- *Salt and pepper*
- *Ground cumin; 1 tsp*
- *Onion powder; 1 tsp*
- *Olive oil; ½ cup*
- *Lime juice; ½*
- *Coriander, ground; 1 tsp*
- *Oregano; 2 tsp*

Method

Take a bowl and mix all the ingredients; herbs and spices well. Place them in a plastic bag and put them in the fridge for 12 hours.

Put the beef in a dehydrator at 165 degrees and let it dry for 6 hours.

Lamb Jerky

Ingredients

- *Pepper*
- *Leg of lamb, sliced; 3 lbs.*
- *Garlic powder; 1 tsp*
- *Worcestershire sauce; 3 tbs*
- *Soy sauce; ¼ cup*
- *Onion powder; 1 ½ tsp*
- *Oregano; 1 tbs*

Method

Take a plastic bag and mix all the ingredients and put them in a plastic-sealed bag. Place it in the fridge for 13 hours.

Set the dehydrator at 145 degrees for 6 hours and place it on the dehydrator tray.

Beef Jerky

Ingredients

- *Beef eye: 2 lbs.*
- *Soy sauce; ½ cup*
- *Salt*
- *Honey; 1 tbs*
- *Worcestershire sauce; ½ cup*

Methods

Slice the beef across the gain. Add soy sauce, salt, honey, and Worcestershire sauce in a plastic bag, add the beef and seal the bag. Coat it well and marinate it in the fridge for 12 hours.

After refrigerating, add the beef to the dehydrator tray and let it process at 165 degrees for 6 hours.

Beef teriyaki jerky

Ingredients

- *Beef round, 2 lbs.*
- *Brown sugar; ¼ cup*
- *Soy sauce; ½ cup*
- *Garlic, crushed; 1 clove*
- *Ginger; ¼ tsp*
- *Pineapple juice; ¼ cup*

Methods

In a bowl, combine all the ingredients. Combine them thoroughly. Place in a plastic bag that can be sealed. Add the plastic bag with the meat.

Marinate for 12 hours in the fridge. Before dehydrating, remove the marinade. Add it to the dehydrator tray and cook for 6 hours at 165 degrees Fahrenheit.

Keep in a glass jar with a lid or vacuum seal for storage.

Vietnamese beef jerky

Ingredients

- *Beef round; 2 lbs.*
- *Fish sauce; 3 tbs*
- *Lime juice; 2 tbs*
- *Brown sugar; ¼ cup*
- *Soy sauce; 1 tbs*

Method

Combine the ingredients one by one in a bowl, mix them well and put this marinated beef in a plastic bag. Let the mixture be in the beef so, and refrigerate it for 12 hours or overnight.

At 165 degrees temperature, set the dehydrator and place the beef on its tray. Process it for 6 hours and store it in an airtight container when done.

Smoked Bacon Jerky with Herbs

Ingredients

- Bacon, smoked; 10 slices
- Fennel seeds, ground; 1 tsp
- Sage, dried; ¼ tsp
- Garlic powder; 1/8 tsp
- Onion powder; 1/8 tsp
- Thyme, dried; ¼ tsp
- Brown sugar; 1 tsp
- Red pepper flakes; ¼ tsp
- Black pepper flakes; 1/8 tsp

Method

Make the three portions of the bacon slices. Take a bowl and mix all the ingredients in it, and whisk them well. When done, on the bacon, sprinkle the seasoning.

On a dehydrator, at 165 degrees F, let it dry and crisp.

Lemon Fish Jerky

Ingredients

- Cod fish fillet, sliced; 1 lb.
- Lemon zest; 1 tsp
- Lemon juice; 1 tbs
- Dill; 1 tsp
- Garlic cloves grated; 1
- Olive oil; 2 tbs
- Salt

Method

Put the fish and the other ingredient in the sealed bag. Shake it well and refrigerate it for 4 hours. Make sure the fish has an equal coating of the mixture all over.

Shake off the extra mixture from the fish and let it dry by placing it on the dehydrator tray. Set the temperature at 145 F for 8 hours.

This can be stored for up to 2 weeks.

Salmon Jerky

Ingredients

- *Salmon, sliced, 1 ¼ lbs.*
- *Lemon juice; 1 tbs*
- *Pepper*
- *Molasses; 1 tbs*
- *Soy sauce; ¼ cup*

Method

Take a sealed plastic bag and place all the ingredients and salmon slices. Mix them separately and add to the bag, ensuring the fish is covered with the seasoning properly.

Place the marinated salmon in the fridge for 4 hours. In the meantime, set 145 degrees F and let it dehydrate for 4 hours.

Fish Teriyaki Jerky

Ingredient

- *Salmon, sliced; 1 lb.*
- *Orange juice; ¼ cup*
- *Garlic clove, minced; 1*
- *Sugar; ¼ cup*
- *Ginger, grated; ¼ teaspoon*
- *Soy sauce; ½ cup*

Method

Take a bowl and mix all the ingredients in it and mix well. In a plastic-sealed bag, add all the ingredients along with the salmon slices. Put this sealed bag in the fridge for 4 hours.

Now, on the dehydrator tray, place the salmon slices on it and at a temperature of 145 F, let it process for 8 hours.

Cajun Fish Jerky

Ingredients

- *Cod fillet, sliced; 1 lb.*
- *Salt and pepper*
- *Garlic powder; 1 tsp*
- *Paprika; 1 tsp*
- *Cayenne pepper; ¼ tsp*
- *Lemon juice; 1 tbs*
- *Onion powder; ` tsp*

Method

In a bowl, add lemon juice, salt, pepper, and other ingredients and mix them well. Season the fish with this mixture and place it in the fridge packed in an airtight bag for a minimum of 4 hours.

Place the fish slices on the dehydrator tray for 8 hours at a temperature of 145 degrees F.

Venison Jerky

Ingredients

- *Venison, roast, and silver skin must be trimmed; 1 lb.*
- *Salt and pepper*
- *Honey; 1 tbs*
- *Onion powder; ¼ tsp*
- *Coconut amino; 4 tbs*
- *Red pepper flakes; ¼ tsp*
- *Worcestershire sauce; 4 tbs*

Method

Cut the venison into slices and place it in a bowl. In another bowl, mix the remaining ingredients, mix them well and pour it on the slices. Let the meat sit in the fridge for a day, and keep flipping it every three to four hours to make the venison rich in flavors.

On a dehydrator at 160 degrees F, let the venison slices dehydrate for 4 hours. This can be stored in a sealed bag for around 3 months and up to 2 weeks in a zip-lock bag.

Hickory Smoked Jerky

Ingredients

- *Beef ground and sliced; 1 lb.*
- *BBQ sauce; ¼ cup*
- *Hickory smoked marinade; ½ cup*
- *Brown sugar; 2 tbs*
- *Salt and pepper*
- *Onion powder; 1 tsp*
- *Cayenne pepper; a pinch*

Method

Place the slices in a sealed bag and add the ingredients into it after mixing them in a bowl separately. Refrigerate it for 12 hours, when done, drain the extra marinade.

On a dehydrator, set the temperature to 180 degrees and let it cook for 4 hours. Do not forget to flip them in between.

Beef Beer Jerky

Ingredients

- *Beef round; 1 lb.*
- *Soy sauce; ½ cup*
- *Garlic cloves, minced; 2*
- *Beer; 2 cups*
- *Honey; 1 tbs*
- *Liquid smoke; 1 tbs*

Method

Put the beef in the plastic seal bag along with the ingredients after mixing them separately in a bowl. Marinate it in the fridge for 6 hours and then place it on the dehydrator tray at 160 degrees temperature for 1 hour first.

After that, turn the temperature down to 150 degrees and dehydrate it for another 4 hours.

Smokey Steak Jerky

Ingredients

- Beef sirloin steak; 1 lb.
- Soy sauce, low sodium; ¼ cup
- Worcestershire sauce; 1 tsp
- Liquid smoke flavor; ½ tsp
- Steak seasoning; 1 tbs
- Brown sugar; 1 ½ tsp

Method

Freeze the beef for an hour and cut it into ¼-inch thick slices. In a bowl, add all the ingredients along with the beef slices and coat them well. Take a sealable bag and transfer the marinated beef in it, and place it in the refrigerator for a minimum of 10 hours to overnight.

After that time, pat the beef with the kitchen towel to remove excess marinade. Now, on the dehydrator tray, place the beef slices into a single layer and let them process at 172 degrees for 4 hours. keep on checking them every 30 minutes and flip them when needed.

When done, remove it from the dehydrator and wrap them in the foil. Set the temperature to 275 degrees in your oven and let it roast for another 6 minutes.

Cajun Pork Jerky

Ingredients

- *Pork tenderloin; 2 lbs.*
- *Old bay seasoning; 1 tbs*
- *Cajun seasoning; 2 tsp*
- *Worcestershire sauce; ¾ cup*
- *Soy sauce; ½ cup*
- *Teriyaki sauce; 1/3 cup*
- *Water; ½ cup*
- *Chili powder; 1 tbs*

Method

Before cutting the slices, place the pork in the fridge for an hour, and slice them ¼ inch afterward. In a bowl, mix all the ingredients and shake them well. Take a sealable bag and add the marinade pork in it and let it sit in the fridge.

With the help of a kitchen towel, pat the slices to soak extra marinade. Place the slices on the dehydrator in a way that they do not overlap. Let it process for 4 hours at 172 degrees.

Chipotle Beef jerky

Ingredients

- *Beef tenderloin; 1 lb.*
- *Chipotle sauce; 7 ounces*
- *Tomato paste; 1 tbs*
- *Brown sugar; 1 tsp*
- *Sea salt; 1 tsp*
- *Garlic powder; 1 tsp*

Method

Freeze the beef for an hour before slicing it. cut the slices into ¼ inch thick and marinade with other ingredients in a large bowl. Mix them all and place them in the plastic bag to marinate overnight in the fridge.

Remove the excess mixture from the slices and place them in the dehydrator. Let it dehydrate for 4 hours at 172 degrees temperature.

Smoked Tofu Jerky

Ingredients

- *Tofu, drained; 1 pack*
- *Soy sauce; 3 tbs*
- *Maple syrup; 2 tsp*
- *Liquid smoke concentrated; ¼ tsp*
- *Garlic powder; 1 tsp*
- *Brown sugar; 2 tsp*
- *Barbecue sauce; 3 tbs*
- *Black pepper; ½ tsp ground*

Method

The tofu recipe is similar to the other meat jerky recipes. Cut it in ¼ inch-thick slices and mix all the ingredients in a large bowl. Place marinated tofu in a sealable bag and put it in the fridge overnight.

Process it on the dehydrator at 172 degrees for 4 hours by placing the slices on the dehydrator tray.

Sriracha Maple beef Jerky

Ingredients

- Beef, sirloin steak; 1 lb.
- Soy sauce; ½ cup
- Maple syrup; ¼ cup
- Sriracha hot sauce; 1 tbs
- Black pepper; ¼ tsp

Method

Freeze the beef before slicing it for firm cutting, make sure they are ¼ inch thick/. In a bowl, add all the ingredients and beef slices, and mix them well. Take a sealable bag and put it all in it, and marinate it overnight or for a minimum of 10 hours. In case you do not have a sealable bag, you can just cover the bowl with a cling.

When marinated, remove the extra mixture and place the slices on the dehydrator tray. Set the temperate at 172 and process it for 6 to 8 hours, check after four hours. When done, cook it in the oven for 6 minutes at 275 degrees after covering it in the foil.

Mesquite Smoked jerky

Ingredients

- Beef, eye round; 1 lb.
- Soy sauce; 1 cup
- Salt
- Garlic cloves, minced; 3
- Paprika, ground; 1 tbs
- Liquid smoke concentrated; 2 tbs
- Packed brown sugar; ½ cup

Method

Slice the beef into ¼ inch thick. Make sure to freeze it first this will cut the beef easily. Mix the ingredients and the beef in a bowl and transfer them into a sealable bag. Marinate overnight.

Place the parchment paper on the dehydrator tray and let it process for 7 to 9 hours at 165 degrees. Flip the strips halfway.

Thai curry Pork jerky

Ingredients

- *Pork tenderloin; 1 lb.*
- *Thai red curry paste; 3 tbs.*
- *Fish sauce; 2 tbs*
- *Water; 2 tbs*
- *Salt*
- *Garlic clove; 1*
- *Red curry paste; 3 tbs*

Method

Take the frozen pork tenderloin and cut it in ¼ inch slices. In a large bowl, add all the ingredients and slices, and mix them well. Place it overnight in the fridge in a sealable bag.

Shake off the extra marinade from the slices and place them on the dehydrator tray in a single layer. Process it at 172 degrees for 6 to 8 hours, flip the slices after 3 to 4 hours.

Pepper cod jerky

Ingredients

- *Cod fillet; 1 lb.*
- *Lemon juice; 1*
- *Salt*
- *Garlic powder; 1 tsp*
- *Black pepper; 1 tsp*
- *Cayenne pepper; ½ tsp*

Method

Cut the cod fillet into ¼-inch thick slices and mix it up will all the other ingredients. Marinate it for at least 10 hours, for better taste, you can put it in the fridge overnight in a plastic bag.

Remove the extra mixture by shaking the slices or use a paper towel to pat it lightly. Place these slices on your dehydrator tray and let them dry for 6 to 8 hours at 172 degrees.

When dried properly, place it in the jar.

Lemon pepper fish jerky

Ingredients

- *Haddock fillets; 1 lb.*
- *Lemon juice and zest; 1*
- *Garlic clove; 1 minced*
- *Salt*
- *Olive oil; 2 tbs*
- *Pepper; 1 tbs*

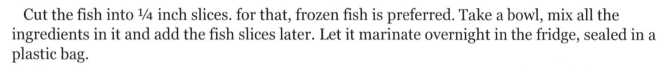

Method

Cut the fish into ¼ inch slices. for that, frozen fish is preferred. Take a bowl, mix all the ingredients in it and add the fish slices later. Let it marinate overnight in the fridge, sealed in a plastic bag.

Take it out and rub off the extra marinade from the fish. Place it on the dehydrator tray and let it dry at 275 degrees for 6 to 8 hours.

Smoked Chicken Jerky

Ingredients

- *Chicken breast and skinless; 1 lb.*
- *Garlic powder; 1 tsp*
- *Ginger powder; 1 tsp*
- *Smoked salt; 1 tsp*
- *Lemon juice: 1 tsp*
- *Soy sauce, low sodium; ¾ cup*
- *Worcestershire sauce; 1 tbs*
- *Black pepper; 1 tsp*
- *Crushed red pepper; 1 tsp*

Method

Cut the chicken strips into ¼ inch thickness and place them in a large bowl along with the other ingredients. Place them in a sealable bag and let the marinade sit in the refrigerator.

When done marinating, bring it out and pat it with the kitchen towel to remove the extra mixture. Place them on the dehydrator tray with distance and let them process for 6 to 8 hours at 165 degrees. flip halfway.

Eggplant jerky

Ingredients

- *Eggplants; 1 lb.*
- *Teriyaki sauce; ½ cup*
- *Water; 2 tbs*
- *Red pepper flakes; ½ tsp*

Method

Wash the eggplants and cut them into slices neither too thick nor too thin. Peel if you want otherwise it is not necessary. Mix all the ingredients in a bowl and marinate the eggplant slices properly.

On the dehydrator, set the temperature at 165 degrees and process it for 5 to 7 hours.

Candied Sweet and bacon jerky

Ingredient

- *Bacon strips; 10*
- *Soy sauce; 3 tbs*
- *Brown sugar; 3 tbs*
- *Garlic chili sauce; 2 tbs*
- *Sesame oil; 2 tbs*
- *Mirin; 2 tsp*

Method

Take the bacon strips and cut them in half. In a bowl combine all the ingredients and mix them thoroughly. Take a sealable bag and place them in it, and let it sit overnight.

On the dehydrator tray, place the bacon strips evenly and process them at 165 degrees for 6 to 8 hours.

Bacon jerky for breakfast

Ingredients

- *Applewood smoked bacon strips; 10*
- *Dried thyme; ½ tsp*
- *Light brown sugar; 1 tsp*
- *Dried sage; ¼ tsp*
- *Onion powder; 1/8 tsp*
- *Fennel seeds, ground; 1 tsp*
- *Red pepper, crushed; ¼ tsp*
- *Garlic powder; 1/8 tsp*
- *Black pepper; 1/8 tsp*

Method

Get the bacon strips and cut them in half. Mix all the ingredients in a bowl and marinade the bacon strips. Sprinkle the seasoning on it and place the strips on the dehydrator tray.

Process it at 165 F for 6 to 7 hours.

Jalapeno Lime Jerky

Ingredients

- *Beef eye round; 2 lbs.*
- *Jalapeno, with seeds; 12*
- *Limes, juiced; 4*
- *Cilantro; 1 cup*
- *Green onion; chopped*
- *Garlic cloves; 2*
- *Salt*
- *Black pepper; ½ tsp*
- *Ground cumin; 1 tsp*
- *Red pepper; 1 tsp*

Method

Cut the beef slices, and make them into 5mm thick slices. In a food processor, blend jalapeno, cilantro, green onion, garlic, cumin, and other remaining ingredients to make a smooth paste. Mix it with beef slices and marinate it by placing it in the refrigerator overnight, wrapped in a plastic bag.

Place it on the dehydrator tray when done at 165 degrees and process it for 6 hours.

Sriracha Honey jerky

Ingredients

- *Beef, eye round; 2 lbs.*
- *Sriracha; 1 cup*
- *Honey; 6 tbs.*
- *Salt*
- *Rice wine vinegar; 4 tsp*

Method

Mix the ingredients and apply them to the beef slices. Seal the marinated beef in a plastic bag and place it in the fridge overnight. When done, drain the extra mixture and place the slices on the dehydrator tray.

At a temperature of 165 degrees, process it for 6 to 8 hours.

Carolina Style Pork Jerky

Ingredients

- *Beef eye round; 2 lb.*
- *Soy sauce; 4 tbs.*
- *Brown sugar; 4 tbs.*
- *Garlic powder; 1 tbs.*
- *Salt*
- *Sesame oil; 1 tbs*

Method

Cut the beef slices, and make them into 5mm thick slices. Mix the ingredients to make a smooth paste. Apply it on beef slices and marinate it by placing it in the refrigerator overnight, wrapped in a plastic bag.

Place it on the dehydrator tray when done at 165 degrees and process it for 6 hours.

Beef Soy Jerky with garlic

Ingredients

- *Beef eye of round; 2 lbs.*
- *Soy sauce; 2/4 cup*
- *Worcestershire sauce; 1 tsp*
- *Garlic powder; 4 tsp*
- *Brown sugar; ¼ cup*
- *Salt*

Method

Cut the beef slices, and make them into 5mm thick slices. Mix soy sauce, Worcestershire sauce, garlic powder, brown sugar, etc. to make a smooth paste. Add beef slices to the mixture and marinate it by placing it in the refrigerator overnight, wrapped in a plastic bag.

Place it on the dehydrator tray when done at 165 degrees and process it for 6 hours.

Jamaican Jerky

Ingredients

- *Beef, eye round, 2 lbs.*
- *Salt; 2 tsp*
- *Black pepper; 2 tsp*
- *Fresh lime; ½ cup*
- *All-specie; 1 tsp*
- *Garlic clove; 4*
- *Ginger; 2 tsp*
- *Dark brown sugar; 2 tbs*
- *Distilled white wine; ½ cup*
- *Smoked paprika; ½ tsp*
- *Onion powder; 2 tsp*
- *Dried thyme; 2 tsp*
- *Cayenne pepper: 1 tsp*
- *Cinnamon; ½ tsp*

Method

Cut the beef slices across grains and make them into 5mm thick slices. Mix the ingredients to make a smooth paste. Apply it on beef slices and marinate it by placing it in the refrigerator overnight, wrapped in a plastic bag.

Place it on the dehydrator tray when done at 165 degrees and process it for 6 hours.

Buffalo Beef jerky

Ingredients

- *Buffalo wing sauce; 1 cup*
- *Salt*
- *Beef, eye round; 2 lbs.*

Method

Take the beef and cut it into 5mm thick slices. Mix the buffalo wing sauce and salt. Apply it on beef slices and marinate it by placing it in the refrigerator overnight, wrapped in a plastic bag.

Place it on the dehydrator tray when done at 165 degrees and process it for 6 1o 8 hours.

Brazilian BBQ Jerky

Ingredients

- *Beef, top round; 2 lbs.*
- *Cumin, ground; 2 tsp*
- *Oregano, dried; 2 tsp*
- *Coriander; ground; 1 tsp*
- *Black pepper; 1 tsp*
- *Olive oil; ½ cup*
- *Lime juice; ½ cup*
- *Salt*
- *Onion powder: 1 tsp*
- *Red pepper crushed; 1 tsp*
- *Garlic cloves, grated; 4*

Method

Cut the beef slices, and make them into 5mm thick slices. Combine the cumin, oregano, onion powder, coriander, salt, pepper, and other ingredients to make a smooth paste. Put on this mixture of beef slices and marinate it by placing it in the refrigerator overnight, wrapped in a plastic bag.

Place it on the dehydrator tray when done at 165 degrees and process it for 6 hours.

Sweet Heat Jerky

Ingredients

- *Beef eye of round; 2 lbs.*
- *Dijon mustard; 4 tbs*
- *Salt*
- *Onion powder; 1 tbs*
- *Chile powder; 1 tbs*
- *Garlic powder; 1 tsp*
- *Cayenne powder; 1 tbs*
- *Smoked paprika; 4 tsp*
- *Brown sugar; 6 tbs*
- *Ketchup; ½ cup*
- *Soy sauce; ½ cup*
- *Worcestershire sauce; ¼ cup*

Method

Cut the beef slices, and make them into 5mm thick slices. Mix the ingredients to make a smooth paste. Apply it on beef slices and marinate it by placing it in the refrigerator overnight, wrapped in a plastic bag.

Place it on the dehydrator tray when done at 165 degrees and process it for 6 hours.

Peppered Jerky

Ingredients

- *Beef, eye round; 2 lbs.*
- *Worcestershire sauce; ¼ cup*
- *White pepper; ¼ tsp*
- *Black pepper; 2 ½ tsp*
- *Soy sauce; ½ cup*

Method

Slice the beef into 5 mm thick, across the grains. Mix the sauces and other ingredients well. Apply it on beef slices and marinate it by placing it in the refrigerator overnight, wrapped in a plastic bag.

Place it on the dehydrator tray when done at 165 degrees and process it for 6 hours.

Smoked Salmon Jerky

Ingredients

- *Salmon; 1 ¼ lb.*
- *Molasses; 1 tbs*
- *Lemon juice, freshly squeezed; 1 tbs*
- *Black pepper; 2 tsp*
- *Liquid smoke; 1 tsp*
- *Soy sauce; 1 ¼ lb.*

Method

Cut the salmon fish into ¼-inch thick slices. in a bowl, mix soy sauce, molasses, lemon juice, pepper, and liquid smoke. Apply it on the fish slices and marinate them by placing them in the refrigerator overnight, wrapped in a plastic bag.

Place it on the dehydrator tray when done at 145 degrees and process it for 8 hours.

Cajun Cod Jerky

Ingredients

- *Alaskan cod filet; 1 lb.*
- *Lemon, juiced; 1*
- *Garlic powder; 1 tsp*
- *Salt*
- *Black pepper; ½ tsp*
- *Onion powder; 1 tsp*
- *Paprika; 1 tsp*
- *Cayenne pepper; ¼ tsp*

Method

Slice the cod fish with ¼ thickness across the grains. Mix the ingredients well and pour them on the fish. Make sure every slice is covered with the mixture. Marinate it by placing it in the refrigerator overnight, wrapped in a plastic bag.

Place it on the dehydrator tray when done at 145 degrees and process it for 8 to 10 hours.

Chapter 7: Nuts, Seeds, & Grains

Dried Beans

Ingredients

- *Fresh beans, any; 1 can or 16 oz*

Method

Soak the beans for an hour or two and remove the shells. In case you are taking canned beans then skip this step. By blanching the beans, pre-heat them and bring them to a boil for a minute and drain the water.

Dry beans at 125 degrees for 9 to 13 hours.

Texas Chili Peanuts

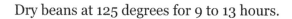

Ingredients

- *Oregano, ground; 1/8 tsp*
- *Cumin, ground; 1 tsp*
- *Peanuts, unsalted and roasted; 1 jar; 16 oz.*
- *Chili powder; 1 ½ tsp*
- *Red pepper; ½ tsp*
- *Water; ½ cup*
- *Hot pepper sauce; ¼ cup*

Method

Combine all the ingredients in the bowl, (nuts must be soaked overnight and drained). Place them on the dehydrator sheet and process them for 3 to 5 hours at 145 degrees.

Maple Chipotle Candied Walnuts

Ingredients

- Raw walnuts, 2 cups
- Cinnamon; ½ tsp
- Maple sugar; finely ground; ½ cup
- Salt
- Chipotle powder; ½ tsp
- Water; 3 to 4 cups

Method

Soak the walnuts in a bowl for 3 to 4 hours. Drain the water and wash them. Take another bowl and mix walnuts will all the other remaining ingredients.

Spread an even layer of well-coated walnuts on the dehydrator tray and process it for 10 hours at 115 degrees.

Make them crispy.

Fruit trail Mix Recipe

Ingredients

- Walnuts; 1 cup
- Dried fruits; 1 cup any and chopped
- Cardamom ½ tsp
- Almonds; 1 cup
- Goji berries; ½ cup
- Hemp seeds; 2 tbs
- Deglet dates, pitted; ½ cup
- Cinnamon; ½ tsp
- Cayenne pepper; 1 pinch
- Raw Mulberries; ½ cup

Method

Dehydrate all the fruits first if they are not dried and soak the nuts for a minimum of 6 hours and chop them. Spread the fruits and nuts on the dehydrator tray and dry them for 2 to 3 hours at 145 degrees.

When done, bring them out, mix all of them and store them in a sealable bag or a glass jar.

Cacao dehydrated almonds

Ingredients

- *Cacao powder; 2 tbs*
- *Raw almonds; 2 cups*
- *Salt*
- *Coconut oil; 1 ½ tbsp*
- *Agave; ¼ cup*

Method

Soak almonds in salted water overnight, drain the water, and air dry them. Mix all the other ingredients into melted coconut oil and pour it on the air-dried almond. Toss them thoroughly.

On a dehydrator tray, spread these coated almonds in a single tray and process for 8 to 12 hours at 125 degrees.

Maple Spiced Pecan

Ingredients

- *Water*
- *Cinnamon; 3 tsp*
- *Maple syrup; ½ cup*
- *Nutmeg; 1/8 tsp*
- *Pecan halve; 3 cups*

Method

Soak pecans in water overnight, drain, wash, and air dry them. When done, toss them with the remaining ingredients so that every piece is coated evenly.

Spread the coated pecans on the dehydrator tray and process them at 105 degrees for 12 to 14 hours. They can be stored for 3 months.

Dehydrated Peanuts

Ingredients

- *Peanuts; 1 bag*

Method

Remove the shells from the peanuts and place them on the dehydrator tray. You can also coat honey or salt if you want.

Spread them on the dehydrator tray and process them at 125 degrees till they become crisp.

Dehydrated Chai Macadamias

Ingredients

- *Himalayan salt; ¼ tsp*
- *Coconut sugar; 1/3 cup*
- *Macadamia nuts; 4 cups*
- *Garam masala; 2 tbs*
- *Cinnamon powder; 2/4 tsp*
- *Vanilla past; 2 tsp*

Method

Soak nuts in the water for 2 hours. in the meantime, take a bowl and mix the other remaining ingredients. This makes the chai powder. Sprinkle them on the nuts when soaked and toss them properly.

Place them in even layers on dehydrator trays; it will fill 2 trays easily without overlapping them. Dehydrate them for an hour at 149 degrees and decrease the temperature to 110 degrees for 16 hours.

Let them cool down before storing them.

Asian Inspired Nuts

Ingredients

- *Ground ginger; ¼ tsp*
- *Water; ¼ cup*
- *Sesame oil; 1 ½ tsp*
- *Soy sauce; 1/3 cup*
- *Five spice powder; ½ tsp*
- *Roasted peanuts; 16 ounces*

Method

Combine and whisk all the ingredients. Add the nuts and mix them. When done, let it rest for a minimum of 8 hours or overnight.

Drain the extra liquids and place them on the dehydrator tray for 5 hours at 135 degrees.

Basic Soaked nuts

Ingredients

- *Nuts, different, in a large quantity*
- *Filtered water; to cover and soak the nuts*
- *Sea salt; 1 tbs for every 4 cups*

Method

Take a bowl, and combine the sea salt, nuts, and water. Cover it with a lid or plate and leave it for 12 hours in a warm cozy place.

After that time, rinse the nuts and place them on the dehydrator tray in a single layer for around 12 to 24 hours by setting the temperature at 105 to 150 degrees.

Orange granola with dried blueberries

Ingredients

- Raw buckwheat or oat groats; 2 cups
- Orange juice, freshly squeezed; 1 cup
- Almond extract; 1 tsp
- Blueberries, dried; ½ cup
- Orange, juiced; 1
- Dates pitted; 1 cup
- Lemon juice; 1 tsp

Method

Soak the groats in water for an hour, drain the water and rinse it well. Put it in a bowl. Take the food processor, add all the ingredients excluding blueberries, and blend it till turns into a paste. Now, add the washed groats, and blend again.

Set 112 degrees at the dehydrator and place the tray with the mixture on it for 12 hours. Flip them and process them for another 15 hours.

When done, cut them into pieces and place the dried berries on the top.

Granola

Ingredients

- Oats, rolled; 3 cups
- Nutmeg; ¼ tsp
- Raw pumpkin seeds; 1 cup raw
- Sunflower seeds; 1 cup raw
- Bran oat; ¼ cup
- Walnuts, pecans, or almonds,
- Cinnamon; 1 tsp
- Coconut; 1 cup
- Honey; ½ cup
- Water; ½ cup
- Coconut oil, melted; ½ cup

Method

Mix honey, water, and coconut oil and add the remaining ingredients afterward. Place them on the dehydrating tray and spread them to create a smooth layer and make a ¼ inch layer.

Dehydrate it for 18 hours at a temperature ranging between 105 to 115 degrees.

Dried and seasoned sunflower seeds

Ingredients

- *Sunflower seeds, raw and shelled; 2 cups*
- *Red pepper flakes, crushed; ¼ tsp*
- *Onion powder; ½ tsp*
- *Garlic powder; ½ tsp*
- *Soy sauce; 1 tbs*
- *Olive oil; 2 tbs*
- *Celery salt; ½ tsp*

Method

Soak the sunflower seeds overnight, drain the water and rinse thoroughly. Mix olive oil, seasonings, and soy sauce and mix them well. Take the seeds and toss them in the mixture.

On a dehydrator tray, place the seeds and let them dry for 12 to 18 hours at 105 to 115 degrees temperature.

Dried sesame seeds

Ingredients

- *Water; 1 cup*
- *Sesame seeds, toasted; ½ cup*
- *Flax seeds; ½ cup*
- *Dried thyme; ½ tsp*
- *Garlic powder; ½ tsp*
- *Sea salt; ½ tsp*
- *Black sesame seeds; ½ tsp*

Method

Take a bowl and mix all the seeds along with the water and stir them well till they are incorporated. Let it sit for 15 minutes till its texture becomes similar to the pudding.

When done, pour the batter onto the dehydrator tray ensuring ¼ inch thickness. Process it for 8 to 12 hours initially and flip them after that time, dehydrate them again for another 8 hours.

Seasoned Cashews

Ingredients

- Roasted cashews; 16 oz.
- Water; ½ cup
- Lime, zested; 1
- Hot sauce; ¼ cup
- Cayenne pepper; ¼ tsp
- Chili powder; 1 ½ tbs
- Fresh lime juice; 3 tbs

Method

In a bowl, add the nuts and ingredients, whisk them well, and let them sit for 8 hours minimum or overnight.

After that time, drain the excess water and spread the nuts on the dehydrator tray. Let them dry got 5 hours at 135 degrees.

Pumpkin seeds with a sweet and salted touch

Ingredients

- Pumpkin seeds; 2 cups
- Olive oil; 2 tbs
- Paprika; 1 tbs
- Ginger, ground; 2 tsp
- Sugar; 1 tbs
- Turmeric; 1 tbs

Method

Take a bowl and put the pumpkin seeds and water in it, making sure the seeds are covered and dipped properly in water. Soak them overnight.

When done, in another bowl, add the seeds and mix them with all the other seasonings—toss them properly to coat them. Spread the seeds on the dehydrator tray at 105 to 115 degrees for 12 to 18 hours.

Sweet Cocoa chia bars

Ingredients

- *Chia seeds; 1 cup*
- *Cocoa powder; ¼ cup*
- *Walnuts, chopped; 1 cup*
- *Figs, chopped; 6*
- *Water; 2 cups*
- *Cacao nibs; 3 tbs*
- *Honey 3 tbs*

Method

Soak the chia seeds in the water for almost 30 minutes, and drain the extra water. Take the food processor and bend all the ingredients excluding cacao nibs. Slowly add the water to maintain the consistency of the mixture.

Now, once it is done, add the chia seeds and cacao nibs to the mixture and put it to rest for 30 minutes. Pour and spread this mixture on the dehydrator tray at 135 degrees for 1 hour, flip them and decrease the temperature to 110, and process it for another 8 hours.

Soaking Nuts & Seeds Dehydrator Recipe

Nuts are difficult to digest due to the enzyme inhibitors while the following process activates the nuts themselves to work. This method can be applied to pistachio, almonds, cashew nuts,

Ingredients

- Filtered Water; A liter or you can adjust it according to the nuts.
- Salt; 1 tbs/liter
- 4 cups of nuts

Method

Take raw nuts and add them to the salted water for a minimum of 7 hours before dehydrating, overnight is preferred. For cashew nuts, 6 hours is the maximum time.

On a dehydrator, set the temperature between 95 to 100 degrees F. Spread the nuts separately on the different trays of dehydrator on top of parchment paper and dehydrate them for 12 to 25 hours. The time for nuts varies on their density.

When they are dry and crispy, store them in an airtight container for weeks. Make sure there is no moisture in the jar or it will spoil the whole batch.

Cacao HEMP Dehydrated energy bars

Ingredients

- *Pitted dates; 1 cup*
- *Raisins; ¼ cup*
- *Goji berry; ¼ cup*
- *Cashew; ¼ cup*
- *Water lukewarm; ¾ to 1 cup*
- *Coconut; 3 tbs shredded*
- *Peeled cacao nibs; 1 cup*
- *Cacao powder; 2 tbs*
- *Hemp seeds; ¼ to ½ cup*
- *Spirulina; 2 tbs*
- *Sesame seeds; 3 tbs*

Method

All the ingredients must be organic. The nuts and raisins must be soaked in water overnight. Dates should be softened by putting them in the water for 20 minutes. Blend them to make a paste.

Blend the other ingredients separately to make them smooth, and mix them both later. On a dehydrating tray, spread the mixture evenly, sprinkle sesame seeds on the top, and let it dry at 135 degrees for 5 to 7 hours.

Seasoned Peanuts

Ingredients

- *Dried roasted and unsalted peanuts; 1 jar*
- *Water; ½ cup*
- *Hot pepper sauce; ¼ cup*
- *Chili powder; 1 ½ tbs*
- *Ground cumin; 1 tsp*
- *Red pepper; ½ tsp*
- *Ground oregano; 1/8 tsp*

Method

Add the layer of peanuts to a 9-inch square pan. In a measuring cup, add all the ingredients and pour them over the nuts layer. Nuts must be soaked overnight at room temperature.

Drain the water and spread it on the dehydrator tray and let it process for 3 to 5 hours at 145 degrees or till they become crisp.

Oriental Cashews

Ingredients

- *Roasted cashew; 12 ounces*
- *Soy sauce; 1/3 cup*
- *Water; ¼ cup*
- *Powdered ginger; ¼ tsp*
- *Garlic powder; 2 tbs*

Method

Take a pan 9-inches and put the nuts. In another bowl, mix all the remaining ingredients and soak them in water overnight. Drain the water and put them on the dehydrating tray.

Let it dry for 3 to 5 hours at 145 degrees till they turn dry and crispy.

Reuben Round Dehydrated

Ingredients

- *Rye flour; 1 ¼ cups*
- *Salt*
- *Caraway seeds; 1 ½ tsp*
- *Swiss cheese, grated; 1 cup*
- *Sauerkraut drained and squeezed*
- *Butter or margarine, softened; ½ cup*

Method

Take a bowl and mix flour, butter, salt, and caraway, and blend them well. Add cheese, and sauerkraut afterward, to a dough.

Make a small ball and cut them into slices. Place it on the wax paper and let it sit for 4 to 6 hours. After that place it on the dehydrator for 4 to 6 hours at 145 degrees.

Reuben Rounds

Ingredients

- Rye flour; 1 ¼ cups
- Salt
- Caraway seeds; 1 ½ tsp
- Butter; ½ cup
- Swiss cheese; 1 grated
- Sauerkraut, drained and squeezed; 1

Method

In a bowl, add flour, caraway seeds, salt, and melted butter, mix them first then add cheese and sauerkraut, and blend them in. Make them all into a dough and in small balls.

Roll it in a log shape by placing it on the wax paper, and let it sit overnight. Next day, cut it in ¼ inch-round slices and dehydrate them at 145 degrees for 4 to 6 hours.

Dehydrated pistachios

Ingredients

- *Pistachios, soaked; 1 cup*
- *Coriander, dried; 1 tsp*
- *Cayenne; ¼ tsp*
- *Maple syrup; 2 tbs*
- *Sea salt; ¼ tsp*
- *Ginger, ground; ¼ tsp*
- *Cinnamon; ¼ tsp*
- *Cumin, ground; ¼ tsp*

Method

Soak the nuts in the water overnight, rinse and set it aside. In a bowl, add maple syrup, coriander, salt, ginger, and other ingredients, and mix them well. add the soaked pistachios and coat them with the seasoning. Toss it well, making sure that every piece is coated properly with the seasonings.

When done, place it on the dehydrator tray and let it dry for 8 to 10 hours at 105 degrees. Store them in an airtight container.

Tamari Almonds

Ingredients

- *Almonds; 1 lb.*
- *Gluten-free tamari; 3 tsp*
- *Water*
- *Sea salt; ½ tsp*

Method

Soak almonds overnight in salted water. Drain and wash them. Pat dry it. in a bowl, add almonds and tamari. Toss them well so they all are coated evenly.

Place them on the dehydrator tray and process them for 12 hours at 100 degrees.

This recipe can be made with any nuts.

PB&J Granola

Ingredients

- *Rolled oats; 2 cups*
- *Dried fruit; 1 cup*
- *Oil; 1 tbs*
- *Hemp; 3 tbs*
- *Buckwheat groats; 3 tbs*
- *Peanut butter; 1 cup*
- *Flax seeds; 3 tbs*
- *Agave or honey; ½ cup*
- *Peanuts, unsalted; 1 cup*

Method

Combine oats, peanuts, flaxseeds; hemp and groats, and dried fruits in a bowl and peanut butter, oil, and honey in another bowl. Microwave the liquids for 30 seconds and stir them well. Pour it over the dried ingredients and make a batter.

Spread it evenly on the dehydrating tray and let it dry for 6 to 10 hours at 115 degrees.

Maple Cinnamon Pumpkin seeds

Ingredients

- *Pumpkin seeds; ¾ cups*
- *Nutmeg; a dash*
- *Salt*
- *Vanilla extract; ½ tsp*
- *Cinnamon; ½ tsp*
- *Maple syrup; 2 tsp*

Method

Rinse pumpkin seeds and soak them overnight. Drain the water and air dry them. In a bowl, put maple syrup, cinnamon, nutmeg, and other ingredients, stir them well and add the soaked seeds later. Toss them thoroughly so that there would no seeds without coating. Let them sit for a while.

Spread the pumpkin seeds on a dehydrator tray and let them process for 20 to 24 hours at 150 degrees.

Dried Granola

Ingredients

- *Dried cherries; ½ cup*
- *Sea salt; a pinch*
- *Raw whole-rolled oats*
- *Maple syrup; 2 tbs*
- *Vanilla extract; ½ tsp*
- *Raw honey; 2 tbs*
- *Applesauce, unsweetened; 1 cup*

Method

In a bowl, mix all the ingredients till they are combined properly and roll them on the drying sheet with a 1/8-inch thickness, then on the dehydrator tray.

Dehydrate it at 125 degrees for 6 to 8 hours. Flip them after halftime. When done, break it into small pieces.

Chili Sunflower seeds

Ingredients

- *Sunflower seeds; 3 cups*
- *Olive oil; 2 tbs*
- *Cumin; 1 tsp*
- *Onion powder; ½ tsp*
- *Tamari; 1 tbs*
- *Brown sugar; 1 tsp*
- *Chipotle or cayenne; a pinch*
- *Garlic minced; 1 clove*
- *Salt*
- *Apple cider vinegar; 1 tbs*
- *Chili powder; 3 tbs*

Method

Soak the seeds in the water for 6 hours, drain, and rinse them. In a bowl, toss them with all the seasoning so they are coated with the ingredients well.

Spread them on a liner placed on the dehydrator tray and let them dry at 115 degrees for 6 to 8 hours.

Pumpkin granola bars

Ingredients

- *Rolled oats; 5 cups*
- *Pumpkin seeds; 1 cup*
- *Flaked coconuts; ¼ cup*
- *Salt*
- *Cinnamon; 2 tsp*
- *Pumpkin pies spice; 1 tbs*
- *Coconut oil; 2 tbs*
- *Organic pumpkin puree; ½ cup*
- *Flax seeds; ¼ cup*
- *Organic pumpkin; ½ cup*
- *Almond; ½ cup*
- *Pecans; ½ cup*
- *Golden raisins; ½ cup*

Method

Mix oats, pumpkin seeds, flax seeds, coconut, almonds, pecans, spices, and salt in a bowl and stir them well. In another bowl, mix maple syrup, coconut oil, and pumpkin puree and whisk it. combine both of them and whisk thoroughly.

On a dehydrator tray, pour evenly this mixture ensuring no air bubbles, and let it process at 115 degrees for 8 to 12 hours.

Crispy Salted Almonds

Ingredients

- *Raw almonds; 15 cups or 3 lbs.*
- *Filtered water*
- *Sea salt; 3 tbs*

Method

Put the almonds in a bowl filled with salt and water, must be covering almost up to 3 inches. Let them soak overnight in the kitchen at room temperature and in a warm place during winter, in an oven.

Drain the water and add a half teaspoon of salt and toss the almonds. Spread it all over the dehydrating tray and process them for 12 hours.

Dehydrated Vegan pistachio Nut cheese

Ingredients

- *Cashew, soaked; 1 cup*
- *Pistachios shelled and soaked; 1 cup*
- *White miso paste; 1 tbs*
- *Garlic powder; 1 tsp*
- *Coconut oil; 1 tbs*
- *Nutritional yeast; 1 tbsp*
- *Aquafaba; ½ cup*
- *Salt*
- *Fresh herbs and pistachios for garnishing*

Method

In a mold of 4 inches, apply coconut oil lightly and set it aside. In a blender, combine all the ingredients and turn them into a smooth paste.

Pour it into the mold and tap gently to remove any space and air in the batter. Place the mold into your dehydrator by removing the extra trays from it.

Let it dry for 24 hours at 90 degrees. When done, garnish it with fresh herbs and pistachios.

Blueberry energy bites

Ingredients

- *Nour dates; 1 ½ pitted*
- *Dried berries; 1/3 cup*
- *Sea salt; ¼ tsp*
- *Vanilla extract; 1 tsp*
- *Almond butter; 2 ½ tbsp*
- *Cashew, almond, or any nuts; 1 cup*

Method

Blend dates, nuts, almond butter, vanilla extract, and sea salt in the food processor for 1 minute to make a consistent mixture. When done, add frozen berries and mix them well.

On a dehydrator tray, place a scoop of batter and flatten it with a tablespoon. Dehydrate it for 6 to 8 hours at 135 degrees.

Sweet and Salted trail mix

Ingredients

- *Melted butter; 3 tbs*
- *Brazilian nuts; 1 cup*
- *Pecans; 1 cup*
- *Almonds; 1 cup*
- *Dried mangoes, chopped; ½ cup*
- *Dried apples, chopped, ½ cup*
- *Pumpkin seeds; ½ cup*
- *Raisins; ½ cup*
- *Dried goji berries; ½ cup*
- *Sea salt; 1 tsp*
- *Pistachios with shells; 1 cup*
- *Walnuts; 1 cup*
- *Sunflower seeds; ½ cup*

Method

Soak all the nuts and seeds separately overnight and drain the water. Put all the soaked nuts and seeds in a bowl, and pour melted butter and a pinch of sea salt. Coat them properly.

Place all the nuts on the parchment paper spread on the dehydrator tray. Process them for 10 to 24 hours at 110 degrees F for 2 hours and then at 95 F for the remaining time.

Sprouted Candied Nuts and seeds

Ingredients

- Coconut sugar; ¼ cup
- Raw nuts or and seeds of your choice; 2 cups
- Orange zest; 1
- Pumpkin spice; 2 tsp
- Egg white; 1
- Sea salt
- Molasses blackstrap; 1 tsp

Method

Soak all the nuts and seeds all together or separately it is up to you. Pour water into the bowl and make sure it must be above it almost 2 inches. Sprinkle sea salt, mix them in water and let it soak overnight.

Take a bowl and whisk the egg, add coconut sugar, and pumpkin pie spice and mix them well. Add soaked nuts after and stir them well to coat the nuts evenly.

Spread them all on a dehydrating tray and process them at 135 degrees for 12 to 24 hours.

Paleo Blueberry Granola

Ingredients

- Water; 1 ¼ cups
- Buckwheat flour; 2 cups
- Fresh berries; 4 cups
- Almond extract; 1 ½ tbs
- Raw honey; 1 to 2 cups
- Sea salt; 2 tsp
- Shredded coconut; 1 lb.
- Melted coconut oil; 1 ½ cups
- Almond flour; 1 ½ cups
- Seeds or nuts of your choice; 4 cups

Method

In a mixing bowl, add buckwheat flour, water, and sea salt and soak them for 10 to 12 hours. When done, drain the extra water and combine all the other ingredients, mix well.

Place it on the dehydrator tray at 135 degrees and process it for 12 to 24 hours. This process can also be done at 165 degrees for 7 to 9 hours if you are running out of time.

Cherry Granola

Ingredients

- *Cherries, fresh and pitted; 6 cups*
- *Rolled oat; 4 cups*
- *Sea salt; 1 tbs*
- *Lemon juice for soaking; 1*
- *Melted coconut oil; 1 cup*
- *Coconut flour; 2 cups*
- *Shredded coconut; 2 cups*
- *Raw walnuts; 2 cups*
- *Pecans, raw; 2 cups*
- *Raw honey; ½ cup*
- *Almond extract; 2 tbs*

Method

Soak all the nuts overnight and drain the water. Pat dry them. Put all the ingredients in a bowl, and add the soaked seeds and nuts. toss them properly.

Scoop the mixture on the dehydrator tray and process it at 135 degrees for 8 to 12 hours.

Pumpkin Granola

Ingredients

- *Rolled oats; 5 cups*
- *Almonds; ½ cup*
- *Pumpkin seeds; 1 cup*
- *Golden raisins; ½ cup*
- *Pecans; ½ cup*
- *Flax seeds; ¼ cup*
- *Salt*
- *Cinnamon; 2 tsp*
- *Flaked coconut; ¼ cup*
- *Organic pumpkin; ½ cup*
- *Maple syrup; ¾ cup*
- *Coconut oil; 2 tbs*
- *Pumpkin pie spice; 1 tbs*

Method

Mix the dry ingredients in a bowl with a spatula and the liquids in another bowl, and mix them too. Now, combine both to make a batter and let them be coated with it thoroughly. Spread them on a dehydrator tray ensuring that they are not overlapping.

Let it dry at 115 degrees for 8 to 12 hours.

Cinnamon Pumpkin Granola

Ingredients

- Oats; 6 cups
- Raw pumpkin seeds; 2 cups
- Buckwheat flour; 2 cups
- Walnuts; 2 cups
- Raw pecans; 2 cups
- Salt
- Pumpkin puree; 15 oz.
- Coconut oil, melted; 1 cup
- Raw honey; ½ to ¾ cup
- Vanilla extract; 1 tbs
- Lemon juice; 1
- Cinnamon powder; 1 to 2 tbs
- Organic molasses; ¼ cup

Method

Make a sticky mixture by adding water, lemon juice, sea salt, walnuts, pecans, pumpkin seeds, buckwheat, and oats. Be sure that the water level must not exceed much. Let it sit overnight.

When done, take a large bowl and add this mixture along with the other ingredients. Balance the sweetness if needed and let it process at 125 degrees for 12 hours. Flip it halfway.

Chapter 8: Fruits, Vegetables, & Leathers

Chocolate Banana Leather

Ingredients

- *Banana; 4*
- *Cocoa powder; 2 tbs*
- *Brown sugar; 1 tbs*

Method

Make a puree of the bananas and add cocoa powder and brown sugar. Mix them well and pour them into the dehydrator tray. Let it dehydrate for 10 hours at 130 degrees, flip them halfway and process it for the rest of the time. make the rolls by scraping them.

Apple fig fruit leather

Ingredients

- *Washed fig; 10 ripe*
- *Apples; 2 cores removed*
- *Orange juice; 1 cup*

Method

In a saucepan, put all the ingredients and bring them to a boil. Let it simmer for a while and reduce the heat for 30 minutes approximately.

When done, blend them to make a puree and pour a thin layer on the dehydrator tray. Let it dehydrate at 125 degrees for 6 to 8 hours.

Dehydrated Chives

Ingredients

- *Chives*

Method

Cut chives into 1 ½ inches and spread them on the dehydrator tray. Let it dry at 95 degrees for 3 to 5 hours.

Strawberry spicy fruit leather

Ingredients

- *Strawberries, chopped and hulled; 1 lb.*
- *Jalapeno or serrano pepper; 1 (without seeds)*
- *Lemon juice; 1 tbs*
- *Granulated sugar; 1/3 cup*

Method

Make the strawberry puree and add lemon juice and pepper.

Mix it well and pour this on the dehydrator tray in strip form with 1/8 inch thickness.

Set the temperature to 140 and let it dry for 6 to 8 hours.

Fruit Leather

Ingredients

- *Peaches, sliced; 3*
- *Apricots; sliced; 3*
- *Sugar; 1 tbs*

Method

Put both fruits in a pot, sprinkle sugar on it, and place it on low-medium heat. When melted, mix them well, bring them off the burner and let them cool.

When done, blend it to make a puree and pour the mixture into a fruit roll sheet and place it on the dehydrator.

Let it dry at 165 degrees for 8 hours. Once it is done, let it cool at room temperature before storing it in a container.

Candy slices of watermelon

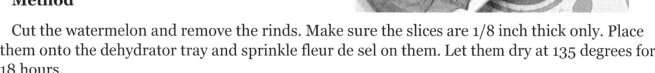

Ingredients

- *Fleur de sel*
- *Watermelon; 1*

Method

Cut the watermelon and remove the rinds. Make sure the slices are 1/8 inch thick only. Place them onto the dehydrator tray and sprinkle fleur de sel on them. Let them dry at 135 degrees for 18 hours.

Honey Peaches with bourbon

Ingredients

- *Peach, sliced with removed core; 1*
- *Bourbon; 3*
- *Honey; ¼ cup*
- *Hot water; ¼ cup*

Method

Put the fruit slices into a sealable bag. Take a bowl and mix honey and hot water till the honey dissolve properly. When done, pour bourbon, whisk it and let it cool, pour it into the bag. For 4 hours, let both of them marinate.

Place these slices after that time on the dehydrator tray at 145 degrees and process them for 16 hours. This can be stored for 10 days.

Raspberry rolls

Ingredients

- *Raspberries; 1 ½ lb.*
- *Sugar; 2 tbs*

Method

Add sugar and raspberries to a food processor and blend them well. Strain the seeds ensuring a smooth puree. Blend it again and make liquid out of it and pour it on a fruit roll sheet. Place it on the dehydrator at 165 degrees for 5 hours.

Apple chips with cinnamon garnish

Ingredients

- *Apples, sliced; 2*
- *Lemon juice; 1 tbs*
- *Cinnamon powder; 2 tsp*

Method

Cut the apple into slices and drizzle lemon juice on them. Arrange these slices on the dehydrator tray at 135 degrees for 6 hours. Store them in a jar and sprinkle cinnamon powder before serving.

Candied Pumpkin

Ingredients

- *Cranberries, chopped; 2 tbs*
- *Coconut flakes; ¼ cup*
- *Coconut milk; 1 cup*
- *Pumpkin puree; 2 cups*
- *Ground cinnamon; ½ tsp*
- *Ground nutmeg; ½ tsp*
- *Allspice; ½ tsp*
- *Honey; ¼ cup*
- *Applesauce; 2 cups*

Method

Take a bowl and mix all the ingredients into it and whisk them. Spread this mixture in the fruit leather sheet of your food dehydrator at 135 degrees and process it for 8 hours.

Strawberry Roll

Ingredients

- *Strawberries; 1 ½ lb.*
- *Sugar; 2 tbs*

Method

Blend strawberries and sugar in a food processor, smooth

it and strain the seeds, blend again. Place this liquid on a food roll sheet.

Put this sheet in the food dehydrator tray at 165 degrees for 5 hours. Store it when dried.

Orange Fruit Leather

Ingredients

- *Applesauce; 1 cup*
- *Vanilla yogurt; 32 oz.*
- *Concentrated orange juice; 1 cup*

Method

In a food blender, add all the ingredients and blend till it

becomes smooth. Place it on the fruit roll sheet of the food dehydrator and let it process at 135 degrees for 6 hours. Do not forget to grease the fruit roll sheet with oil before processing it.

Sweet Dried Lemon

Ingredients

- *Lemon, sliced; 2*
- *Honey or sugar (powdered); 1 tbs*

Method

Arrange the lemon slices at distance on your dehydrating

tray and drizzle sugar or honey whatever you like on the top. Process it at 125 degrees for 6 hours.

Blueberry roll

Ingredients

- *Blueberry roll; 1 ½ lb.*
- *Sugar; 2 tbs*

Method

Take a food processor and add both ingredients to make

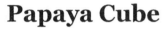

them smooth. Strain it to avoid seeds and blend again to

make it liquid. When done, place it on the fruit roll sheet

and transfer it to a dehydrator tray. Set the temperature to 165 and dehydrate it for 5 hours.

Papaya Cube

Ingredients

- *Papaya, diced; 2*

Methods

Cut the papaya into dice shapes and place it on the

dehydrator tray. Process it at 135 degrees for 12 hours. Save in an airtight jar.

Kiwi Chips

Ingredients

- *Kiwis, peeled and sliced, 2 kiwis*

Methods

Cut the kiwis into slices and place them on the Dehydrator tray. Set the temperature to 136 degrees and process them for 12 hours. Remember, while cutting the kiwi slices, make sure they are 6 mm thick minimum.

Lemon dip Apple Chips

Ingredient

- *White sugar; 1 tbs*
- *Lemon juice; 2 tbs*
- *Apples, sliced; 2*
- *Ground cinnamon; 1 tsp*
- *Nutmeg; ¼ tsp*

Method

Take a bowl and mix all the ingredients except

Apple slices and lemon juice. Dip the slices and put the apple slices on the tray and season them with the mixture.

Place them on the dehydrator tray and set the temperature to 145 degrees. Let it process for 6 hours.

Grapefruit with plum leather

Ingredients

- *Sugar; 2 tbs*
- *Plums, sliced; 5*
- *Red grapes, seeds removed; 2 cups*

Method

Take a pot and put all the ingredients on low to medium heat and let it cook for 15 minutes. When done, let it cool for a while and then place it in a blender to make it smooth liquid. Pour this blended mixture on the fruit roll sheet and place it in your dehydrator at 165 degrees to process for around 12 hours.

Berry Fruit leather with Vanilla extract

Ingredients

- *Strawberries; 1 lb.*
- *Vanilla extract; 1 tsp*
- *Raspberries; ½ cup*
- *Sugar; 2 tsp*

Method

Make a smooth puree by blending the berries in a food processor. Strain it after a while to remove the seeds and blend again to bring it to liquid form.

Pour this mixture on the fruit roll sheet and put it tray in the dehydrator. At 165 degrees, make puree leather for 6 hours.

Sprinkle the sugar when done.

Dried Strawberries

Ingredients

- *Strawberries, sliced; 1 lb.*

Method

The recipe is simple. cut the thin slices of strawberries

and process them at 135 degrees till they become crisp for 8 hours straight.

Hazelnut banana leather

Ingredients

- *Chocolate hazelnut spread*
- *Banana, peeled and sliced; 2*

Method

In a food processor, add banana slices and chocolate hazelnut spread, and blend them well till become smooth. On parchment paper, form ¼-inch thick round shapes of the puree and place it in the dehydrator. Let it dehydrate and become crispy at 125 degrees for 4 hours.

Apple fruit leather

Ingredients

- *Salt*
- *Cinnamon powder; 1 tsp*
- *Honey; ¼ cup*
- *Applesauce; 2 cups*
- *Sweet potatoes, cooked and mashed; 2 cups*

Method

Blend all the ingredients in a food processor and bring it until becomes smooth. Pour it on the fruit roll sheet of the dehydrator and let it dry at 100 degrees for 6 hours.

In case you find it too sweet, add a bit of lemon juice to balance the flavor.

Banana and peanut butter leather

Ingredients

- *Peanut butter; 2 tbs*
- *Banana; peeled and sliced; 2*

Method

Process both ingredients in a food processor and bring them to the puree for at least 1 minute. On the dehydrator tray, place the sheet and pour the mixture. Let it dry at 135 degrees for 4 hours.

Sweet and sour cranberries

Ingredients

- *Orange and lime zest; 1 each*
- *Corn syrup/ sugar ¼ cup*
- *Cranberries; 12 oz.*

Method

Put the cranberries in the bowl and cover them with hot boiling water to crack the skin. When done, toss the berries with the other ingredients.

Put the mesh of the berries on the sheet and freeze it for 2 hours. Dehydrate it at 135 degrees and assemble the mesh on the tray for 12 to 16 hours to bring a chewing texture.

Caramelized Apples

Ingredients

- *Apples, granny smith; 3 to 4*
- *Caramel sauce, store-bought; ½ cup*

Method

Wash and slice the apples in a round shape and remove the core. With the help of a pastry brush, apply caramel in a small amount on each slice. Place them on the dehydrator tray and dehydrate the apple slices at 135 degrees for 10 to 12 hours.

Sweet Potato and Cinnamon leather

Ingredients

Sweet potatoes; 3 medium

- *Cinnamon; ½ tsp*
- *Ground ginger; 1/8 tsp*

Method

Bake the sweet potatoes in an oven at 400 degrees pre-heated oven and let them cook for 35 to 45 minutes. When done, peel the skin and process it in a blender with cinnamon and ginger—blend it till it becomes smooth.

On the dehydrator tray, pour the puree with ¼ inch thickness and let it crisp for 8-6 hours at 135 degrees.

Tangy Mangoes

Ingredients

- *Mangoes, ripe; 4 to 5*
- *Lime juice; ¼ cup*
- *Salt*
- *Honey; 1 tbs*

Method

Peel and slice the mangoes into strips form. Take a bowl and dissolve honey and lime juice in it, and dip the fruit slices in it. Make sure the excess juice is removed.

Place these slices on the dehydrator tray at 135 degrees and let them process for 8 to 9 hours.

Tropical Pineapple chips

Ingredients

- *Pineapple, ripe; 1*
- *Coconut oil*
- *Sea salt*
- *Sweetened coconut flakes; ½ cup*

Method

Peel and cut the pineapple, remove the core, and cut them into round slices ½ inch thick. Apply coconut oil on the slices with the help of a pastry brush and sprinkle the coconut flakes on them along with the sea salt.

Set the dehydrator tray, set the temperature at 135 degrees, and dehydrate them for 12 to 16 hours. Flip the slices halfway.

Apple with nuts and raw cereal

Ingredients

- *Apple juice; 3 tbs*
- *Maple syrup; ¼ cup*
- *Salt*
- *Apple, peeled, seed removed, cut in dice;*
- *Millet flour; ½ cup*
- *Flax seeds, ground; ½ cup*
- *Walnuts, raw; ½ cup*
- *Wheat berries, sprouted, 1 cup*
- *Coconut oil; ¼ cup*
- *Cinnamon; 1 tsp*
- *Sunflower seeds; ½ cup*

Method

Take a blender and whisk coconut oil, maple syrup, and apple juice. In a bowl, combine the remaining ingredients, mix them well, and slowly add the blended liquids in it. stir well.

When done, dehydrate the mixture to make it crisp for 18 to 24 hours at 115 degrees. Once dried, cut or break it into pieces.

Banana Crepes for breakfast

Ingredients

- *Banana, ripe; 2*
- *Cinnamon*
- *Almond milk; 1 tsp*
- *Almond meal; 1 tsp*
- *Ground flax seed; 1 tsp*

Method

Bring these ingredients to the liquid form and blend them into liquid. When done, place them on the dehydrator sheet and pour the mixture on it—spread it with the help of a spatula. This must not be thick than 1/8 inch.

At a temperature of 115, dehydrate it for 3 hours. Make sure the crepes are smooth and must be done properly. Cut them into circles.

Nuts and fruit balls

Ingredients

- *Flaked coconut; 1 cup*
- *Cranberries, dried; ½ cup*
- *Pecan, crushed; 1 cup*
- *Coconut oil; 3 tsp*
- *Almonds, crushed; 1 cup*
- *Cherries, dried; ½ cup*
- *Apricots, dried; ½ cup*
- *Date, dried; ½ cup*
- *Figs; ½ cup*

Method

Process the dates, figs, apricots, cranberries, and cherries in the blender. Slowly add coconut oil and nuts to a bowl. Mix them well to give them a dough-like texture and make small balls.

Let them dehydrate at 135 degrees for 6 hours.

Nut cluster with fruits

Ingredients

- *Rolled oats, raw; 1 cup*
- *Cashew butter; ½ cup*
- *Cinnamon; 1 ½ tsp*
- *Dates pitted; 8*
- *Salt*
- *Rolled oats; 1 cup*
- *Vanilla extract; 1 tsp*
- *Maple syrup; ½ cup*
- *Cranberries, dried; 1 cup*
- *Blueberries, dried; 1 cup*
- *Pecans; 1 cup*

Method

Combine cashew butter, maple syrup, vanilla extract, salt, cinnamon, and date. Make a smooth mixture. Add the other ingredients separately in the bowl, mix them and add the liquid mixture, tossing properly.

Pour this mixture into the dehydrator sheet and dry it for an hour at 145 degrees and then decrease the temperature to 115 and process it for another 24 hours.

Vanilla-apricot slice

Ingredients

- Apricots, 7 to 9 medium-sized, pitted
- Warm water; 4 tbs
- Vanilla bean seeds; scraped
- Honey; 1 ½ tsp

Method

Take a bowl and add honey and vanilla seed, mix with

warm water until the seeds are separated. Cut apricots into slices and place them on the dehydrator tray.

With the help of a brush, apply the vanilla solution to them and process them at 135 degrees for 9 to 12 hours.

Dehydrating Mushroom

Ingredients

- *Mushroom; washed and sliced; ½ lb.*

Method

Wash and cut off the mushrooms and slice them into 1/8 inch. Place them on a dehydrator tray in a single layer and process them at 125 degrees for 6 to 8 hours.

When done, store them in a jar.

Dried Zucchini

Ingredient

- *Zucchini, sliced and cut into slices; 3 to 4*

Method

Wash and cut zucchini into 1/8-inch thick slices in whatever

The shape you like. At a temperature of 135 degrees F,

dehydrate it for 8 hours.

Dehydrating Spinach

Ingredients

- *Spinach; 1 bunch or pack*

Method

Spinach leaves are a lot more spacious so instead of single layering, you can make two. Place washed spinach on the dehydrator tray, and make sure the water droplets are not dripping from the leaves.

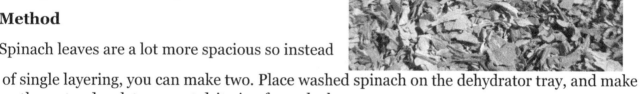

At a temperature of 125 degrees, dry them for 6 hours. After two hours, spread them to a single layer as the leaves will shrink.

Tip: due to drying, they might begin to blow so place a mesh sheet on them.

Dried Sauerkraut

Ingredients

- *Sauerkraut, 7 oz.*

Method

Place the sauerkraut on a dehydrating tray and set the temperature to 125 degrees.

Let it dry for 4 to 6 hours. stir in between.

Dehydrating Steamed vegetables

Some vegetables are hard enough that they need to be steamed first. Before dehydrating, put these mentioned vegetables in the water and bring them to a boil until they turn soft. You can also add a pinch of salt. What else to do, here are the recipes.

Dried Broccoli and Cauliflower

Ingredients

- *Broccoli head rinsed and grit removed; 1*
- *Cauliflower head girt and rinsed; 1*

Method

Wash and cut the cauliflower into ½ inch chunks and cut the bottom. Steam both of them before putting them on the dehydrator tray.

Put the non-stick sheet on the dehydrator tray and place the vegetable florets on it. Set the temperature to 125 and process it for 8 hours.

Carrot Sticks

Ingredients

- *Carrots, core removed, steamed; 2 lbs.*
- *Salt and pepper*

Method

Wash the carrots, cut them into sticks 1 ½ inches long, and remove the core. Steam the carrots and put them in a bowl—season with salt and pepper and toss them. Let they cool at room temperature. When cooked, on a dehydrator tray, place these sticks and dehydrate them at 125 degrees to 135 degrees, depending on the thickness of the carrot. Process it for 6 to 10 hours.

When done, place them in an airtight container.

Corn Dehydrating on the cob

Ingredients

- *Corn with cob; 10 to 12*

Method

You can dry the steamed corn straight on the mesh sheet but there are chances that some of them may fall through. Drying the corn without the non-stick sheets is better as it will improve the airflow in the dehydrating process.

Spread the corn on the dehydrator tray in a single layer and dry it at 5 125 degrees for 6 to 9 hours.

Dehydrating green beans

Ingredients
- *Green beans, fibrous; ½ lb.*

Method
Take a bowl and place the beans into it. Wash them properly to remove dirt and let them dry a bit. Cut the beans into 1 to 2 inches in length and steam them. When done, let them cool to room temperature. Place them on the dehydrating tray, process and them for 8 hours by setting the temperature at 125 degrees.

Dehydrating Potatoes

Ingredients
- *Potatoes, washed and sliced/diced; 2 lbs.*

Method
Wash the potatoes thoroughly and cut them into either slices or dice them. They must not be thick more than 1/8 inch and ¾ inch if dicing. Spread them on a dehydrator tray in a single layer and let them dehydrate for 8 hours at 125 degrees. They will turn hard when dried.

Spicy Mango Fruit Leather

Ingredient

- *Mangoes; 2*
- *Cayenne pepper; ¼ tsp*
- *Lime juice, squeezed; 2 tsp*
- *Maple syrup; 1 tbs*

Method

Peel and remove the core from the mangoes.

In a food processor, put the maple syrup, mangoes, and lime juice in a blender. Make a puree and filter it through a mesh filter.

On the fruit roll sheet, spray the non-stick spray and put the puree on it. With the help of a spatula, spread it all over and flatten it. Place the tray in the dehydrator for 6 to 10 hours to dehydrate at 165 degrees.

Blackberry Chile fruit leather

Ingredients

- Blackberries, fresh, 1 or 2 lbs.
- Serrano pepper, chopped; 2
- Granulated sugar; 1/3 cup
- Salt
- Squeezed lime juice; 3 tsp

Method

In a blender, add blackberries, sugar, and pepper and mix them well. Filter the puree with a mesh filter. On medium heat, cook the puree by stirring it occasionally, bringing it to a boil, or till it turns a bit thick. Turn off the heat and let it cool.

When done, pour it on the tray and flatten it with a rubber spatula. Let it dehydrate at 165 degrees for 6 to 10 hours.

Black and Blueberry fruit leather

Ingredients

- *Blueberries; 1 lb.*
- *Blackberries; ½ cup*
- *Maple syrup; 1 tbs*

Method

Blend all the ingredients and make a smooth puree.

Filter it through a mesh strainer with the help of a

rubber spatula. On the fruit roll sheet, spray non-stick spray and pour the puree. Spread it all over evenly and place the tray in the dehydrator.

Process it at 165 degrees for 6 to 10 hours almost. Make sure the puree is dried properly from the middle.

Grape Maple fruit leather

Ingredient

- *Plum; 6*
- *Grape; seedless*
- *Maple syrup; 1 tsp*
- *Water; ½ cup*

Method

Peel and remove the core of the plums. Cook plums

and grapes at low flame for a minimum of 15 minutes or till they turn soft. When done, blend them all at a low speed and filter them to make a smooth puree.

Set the temperature to 165 and dehydrate it for 6 to 10 hours.

Dehydrating Sweet Pepper

For dehydrating this fruit, sweet bell pepper is one of the easiest ways.

Ingredients,

- Bell pepper; washed, cut properly, and de-seed

Method,

Cut the bell pepper into strips and half. Make sure they are washed properly and place them on single later dehydrator sheets. Set the dehydrator at 125 to 135 degrees till it gets crisp, it will take around 12 to 24 hours and even more. Try not to cut the smaller pieces. Once they are done, they are ready to store and they will shrink to three cups and lasts for one year in the pantry.

You can always rehydrate by simply putting it in the thing that you are cooking without boiling or doing anything else.

Chapter 9: Vegan Dehydrated Recipes

Dehydrating tofu

Ingredients

- *Tofu*

Method

Tofu is available in a variety of textures firm, semi-firm, or extra firm. Select the one that you like the most and drain the water from it.

Cut them into slices neither thick nor thin. Place the on the dehydrator tray in a single layer and dehydrate them for 3 to 6 hours at 155 degrees.

Dehydrated tofu chicken

Ingredients

- *Tofu; 250 g*
- *Precooked Chicken; 1 breast piece*
- *Seasonings any*

Method

Take firm tofu or freeze it for a while so that it can be cut firmly. Slice it afterwards to dehydrate it or you can cut it in small chunks. Place them in a bowl and mix with the seasoning any that you like. Shred the precooked chicken and add it afterward.

Line the dehydrator tray with the parchment sheet and place the chicken-tofu mixture on the dehydrator tray. Process it at 135 degrees for 8 hours.

Red lentil chili

Ingredients

- Oil; 1 tbs
- Onions; 1 cup diced
- Bell pepper; 1 diced
- Salt
- Garlic cloves; 5
- Zucchini, sliced; 2 cups
- Chili powder; 3 tbs
- Cumin ground; 1 tbs
- Roasted diced tomatoes; 1 can of 14 oz.
- Kidney beans; 1 can of 14 oz.
- Tomato paste; 2 tbs
- Vegetable broth; 2 cups
- Red lentils; 1 cup
- Sugar; 1 tsp

Methods

Heat the oil in the pan and saute the salt, onions and pepper. Let them turn golden and then add zucchini and cook till it softens. Mix them well and add garlic, cumin, and chili and cook for 30 seconds.

Next add tomatoes, beans, broth and stir them till they combine. Let it simmer and add lentils afterward. Simmer it for 20 minutes too till the lentils softens. Add sugar next and stir again.

When done spread it on the dehydrator tray lined with the parchment sheet in a thin layer. Let it dehydrate at 135 degrees for 8 to 12 hours.

Dried Thai green curry

Ingredients

- *Dried rice; precooked; ½ cup*
- *Dried ground chicken; ¼ cup or* Tofu in case you are vegan
- *Dried vegetable, mixed; ¼*
- *Green curry paste; ¼ cup dried*
- *Coconut milk powder; 3 tbs*

Method

Dehydrate the curry paste on at 135 degrees for 6 to 7 hours.

Prepare the chicken according to the Thai green curry. As an alternative, you can also use tofu for chicken. Combine all the ingredients in a water and soak them for 5 minutes and bring them to a boil. Transfer them to an insulated cozy and let them incorporated for 15 minutes.

Thai red curry

Ingredients

- *Dried rice; ½ cup*
- *Dried tofu; ¼ cup*
- *Mixed vegetables; ½ cup*
- *Dried red curry paste; ¼ cup*
- *Coconut milk powder; 3 tbs*
- *Water to rehydrate; 2 cups*

Method

Spread the curry paste on the dehydrator tray and dry for 6 to 7 hours at 135 degrees. Combine all the ingredients in water and soak for 5 minutes. Bring them to a boil and transfer them to an insulated cozy. Let them incorporated for 15 minutes.

Eggfruit lemon curd

Ingredients

- *Medium eggplant; 1*
- *Granulated sugar; ¾ cup*
- *Vegan butter, 2 tbs melted*
- *Lemon zest, 2/3 cup*
- *Potato starch; 1 tbs*
- *Vanilla extract; ½ tsp*
- *salt*

Method

Take the eggplant and peel it. in a blender process it with the other ingredients and make them a puree. line a dehydrator tray and line with a non-stick sheet. Pour the mixture on it as it is or you can pour it in a piping bag and make droplets.

Dehydrate at 110 degrees for 12 hours.

Dried Coconut bacon

Ingredients

- *Coconut flakes; 2 cups*
- *Olive oil; 1 tbs*
- *Braggs liquid amino; 1 tbs*
- *Maple syrup; 1 tbs*
- *Apple cider vinegar; 2 tsp*
- *Liquid smoke; 1 tsp*
- *Smoked paprika; 1 tsp*
- *Salt*

Method

Mix all of the ingredients thoroughly in a big bowl along with the coconut flakes. With the help of your hands to gently mix the ingredients so that the flakes and properly infuse the marinade into them.

Spread these flakes on the dehydrator sheet and process them at 125 degrees for 12 to 24 hours. when done, allow them to cool so they become crispy properly.

Vegan and unstuffed peppers

Ingredients

- *Dried rice; ½ cup*
- *Dried green lentil chill; ¼ cup*
- *Dried bell pepper; ¼ cup*
- *Carrots; 1 tbs; dried*
- *Zucchini, dried; 1 tbs*
- *Tomato sauce leather; 2 tbs*
- *Water to rehydrate*

Method

Dehydrate precooked rice. Combine all the ingredients and let the water soak for 5 minutes. On a light flame and bring them to boil for a minute. Pour it in an insulating cozy. Allow to sit for another 20 minutes or even more if you have time.

Tomato bisque

Ingredients

- *Olive oil; 1 tbs*
- *Yellow onion; 1 medium*
- *Garlic cloves; 3 minced*
- *Salt*
- *Vegetable stock; 4 cups*
- *Fire-roasted crushed tomatoes; 1 can of 28 oz.*
- *Sun dried tomatoes; ½ cup*
- *Raw cashews; ½ cup*
- *Nutritional yeast; 2 tbs*
- *Balsamic vinegar; 1tbs*
- *Black pepper, ground; ½ tsp*
- *Julienned fresh basil; ½ cup*

Method

In a pressure cooker, heat the oil and set them on the saute function. Add onions and garlic cook till tender, it will take 5 minutes and sprinkle salt. Continue cooking for 10 minutes and evenly brown and caramelize.

Pour in the vegetable stock, both kinds of tomatoes, cashews, nutritional yeast, vinegar, and black pepper. Cook in the pressure for 8 minutes and release the steam. Allow it to cool and blend in the processor to make smooth puree.

Pour it on the silicon mesh lined on the dehydrator tray and process at 135 degrees for 8 to 10 hours.

Mango salsa couscous salad

Ingredients

- Couscous; 1 cup
- Water; 1 ½ cup
- Dehydrated mango; 2/3 cup
- Prepared salsa; ¾ cup
- Ground cumin; 2 tsp
- Curry powder; 1 tsp

Method

Dehydrate mangoes and bring them to a boil. Stir in the couscous, salsa, mango, cumin, and curry powder. Put a lid on the top and simmer it on a low heat till water is absorbed completely. Remove from heat and allow to combine for 5 to 10 minutes.

Tomato sauce leather

Ingredients

- Tomatoes, canned; 6 of 14.5 oz.
- Salt; 2 tsp
- Sugar; 2 tsp
- Garlic powder; 1 tbs
- Onion powder; 1 tsp
- Pepper; ½ tsp
- Red chili flakes; 1 tsp
- Dried basil; 1 ½
- Dried oregano; 2 tsp
- Dried parsley; 2 tsp
- Bay leaves; 4
- Red wine vinegar; 2 tbs

Method

In a blender, make a smooth puree by adding the canned tomatoes. Pour it in a pan and bring it to a boil on a medium flame. Reduce heat and simmer it. stir all the ingredients in it. this will take an hour to 1.5 hours.

Spread a thin layer on the dehydrator tray lined with a non-stick sheet. Dehydrate for 6 to 8 hours at 135 degrees.

Lemongrass basil stuffed mushroom

Ingredients

- *Cremini mushroom; 2 lbs.*
- *Olive oil; 2 tbs*
- *Onion; 1 medium*
- *Cauliflower; florets; 1 lbs.*
- *Lemon grass basil sauce; 1, 7 oz.*
- *Tahini; 2 tsp*
- *Nutritional yeast; 2 tbs*
- *Salt*
- *Black pepper; ¼ tsp*
- *Basil minced; 2 tbs*
- *Lemon zest; 1*

Method

Line a parchment sheet on the baking tray and preheat the oven at 350 degrees. Remove mushroom stems and combine the caps with oil in a bowl. Place the coated mushrooms on the baking sheet and bake for 15 minutes or till cooked and soft. Remove the trays from the oven, pour off any extra liquid. Put them aside.

In the meanwhile, preheat a medium pot. Combine the onion and garlic with the remaining and cook for 4 to 5 minutes till golden brown. While thoroughly incorporating, add the sauce and cauliflower. Simmer for 8 to 10 minutes over medium-low heat and cook till tender. Allow to cool and then transfer the food processor, pulse till become smooth batter.

Pour this batter on the dehydrator tray lined with a non-stick sheet. Allow it to dehydrate at 145 degrees for 4 to 8 hours.

Dehydrated Vegan Chestnut Rice

Ingredients

- *Precooked Short grain brown rice; 2 cups*
- *Water; 2 ½ cups*
- *Salt; ½ tsp*
- *Shell chestnuts; 1 cup chopped*
- *Vegan butter; 2 tbs*
- *Toasted black sesame seeds; 1 tbs*
- *Oil; 2 tbs*
- *Vegetable bouillon; 3 cups*

Method

Remove the shelled chestnut. In a pan, heat oil and toss the precooked rice with all the other ingredients and vegetable bouillon. Let them simmer till the rice absorbs. Allow it to cool.

Spread this on the non-stick sheet placed on the dehydrator tray and process at 135 degrees to 8 to 10 hours.

Asparagus and mushroom crepe

Ingredients

- *Flax seed flour; 1 cup*
- *Water; ½ cup*
- *Coconut oil; 1 tsp*
- *Light agave nectar; 1 tsp*
- *Salt*

Filling

- *Olive oil; 1 tbs*
- *Asparagus; 1 bunch*
- *Shiitake mushroom caps; 6 to 8 sliced*
- *Garlic clove; 1*
- *Salt and pepper*

Method

To make crepe, mix all the ingredients to make batter, till smooth with as much water as required. in a pan, saute the ingredients listed for filling for a medium heat till the vegetables are tender then add seasonings; salt and pepper.

Now, for the batter, take a pan with a flat bottom, grease it lightly with oil and then whip it. on the low heat, pour the batter and place some filling on it when half done. cover the filling by flapping the craps from both sides and secure it. make sure the filling would not leak.

When it is done, cut it in thin slices. Line the dehydrator tray with parchment paper and place these slices on it. dehydrate at 145 degrees for 8 hours.

Avocado cauliflower rice

Ingredients

- Steamed Cauliflower head; half, boiled
- Avocado; 1.5 oz.
- Lime juice; 2 tsp
- Garlic powder; 1/8 tsp
- Salt; ¼ tsp
- Cilantro; ¼ cup
- Precooked short rice; 1 cup
- Water

Method

Mash the avocados and set them aside. Steam the cauliflower. Heat a pan and add mashed avocado and steamed cauliflower. Saute and add garlic powder, cilantro, a little water and lime juice. Cook them a for a minute and add precooked rice afterward. Mix them well, cover with a lid. Turn the flame to low and simmer till the water is dried. When done, remove from heat and let them cool.

Process them further by spreading them on a dehydrator tray lined with parchment sheet. Dehydrate them for 8 hours at 145 degrees

Dehydrated Pemmican

Ingredients

- Ground meat; 454 g.
- Salt
- Herbs and spices; 2 tbs
- Beef tallow, melted; 454 g

Method

Melt tallow in the oven at 350 degrees for 10 minutes. Take a bowl and mix the remaining ingredients. When the tallow is melted, bring it to the room temperature and moisten the mixture with it. make a consistent paste with it by mixing it well.

When done, spread it on the dehydrator tray lined with a non-stick sheet and process it for 8 to 10 hours till at 135 degrees. Flip and cut them in bars after an hour have passed.

Spicy tomato gnocchi

Ingredients

For tomato sauce

- *Tomato powder; 1 tbs*
- *Chili flakes; ¼ tsp*
- *Dried parsley; ¼ tsp*
- *Oregano dried; ¼ tsp*
- *Basil dried; ¼ tsp*
- *Garlic salt; 1/8 tsp*
- *Shallot; ½ tsp*
- *Parmesan cheese; 1 tsp*
- *Sugar; a pinch*
- *Ground pepper; a pinch*

For Gnocchi

- *Instant mashed potatoes; 2/3 cup*
- *Plain flour; 1/3 cup*
- *Powdered egg; ½ tsp*
- *Dried parsley; ½ tsp*
- *Salt; 1 pinch*
- *Garlic powder; 1/3 pinch*
- *Water; 1/3 cup*

Method

Dehydrate eggs, parsley, pepper, basil, and oregano according to their respective dehydrating time. Pour the water slowly into the gnocchi bag, squeeze it to combine the flour mixture into a dough.

To create a malleable, soft dough, squeeze and compress the bag until all the ingredients are blended and moshed together. Bring 2 cups of water to boil. Make gnocchi piping bag trim about 2 cm off of one of the bottom corners of the dough bag.

Squeeze the dough through the opening, then slice off 2 cm-long pieces and drop them into the hot water. Drain the liquid from the saucepan after the gnocchi float to the top (1 to 3 minutes), leaving 1/2 cup behind. Minimize the heat to low.

Taco-seasoned beyond burger tortillas

Ingredients

- *Dried taco-seasoned beyond burger; ½ cup*
- *Tortilla; 1 or 2 tortillas*
- *Water to rehydrate; ¼ cup*

Method

Add dry Beyond Burger crumbles after bringing water to a boil. Since rehydration occurs quickly, turn off the stove. One or two tortillas should be rolled up or folded over rehydrated crumbs. When adding the burger crumbles, rehydrate any additional dry veggies, beans, or rice first because they will take longer to rehydrate.

Dehydrated Beef burger chili

Ingredients

- *Ground beef burgers; 1 lb.*
- *Onion; large; 1*
- *Garlic clove; 2 to 3*
- *Corn; 1 cup*
- *Red kidney beans; 1 can*
- *Diced tomatoes;*
- *Chili mix powder; 3 tbs*
- *Salt to taste; ½ tsp*
- *Oil; 2 tbs.*

Method

Saute onion and garlic in heat oil in a pan on medium flame and add ground beef. cook till it turns brown. Mix rest to the ingredients one by one and let it cook in water loose by tomatoes. Cover with lid and allow to simmer at low flame. When done, remove from heat and bring it to room temperature.

Pour and spread the mixture on the dehydrator tray lined with parchment paper and dry it at 145 degrees for 8 hours.

Textured vegetable protein chili dehydrated

Ingredients

- *Dried Beef-Flavor TVP: 1 ½ cup*
- *Warm water; 1 ½ cup*
- *Red beans; 1 can*
- *Tomatoes, diced; 1 can*
- *Onion, small; 3*
- *Garlic cloves; 2*
- *Carrot; 1 diced*
- *Pepper; 1 bell*
- *Chili mix powder; 3 tbs*
- *Tomato paste; 3 tbs*
- *Dried parsley; 2 tbs*
- *Salt; 1 ½ tsp*
- *Cumin; 1 tsp*
- *Water; 1 ½ cup*

Method

In a dish, rehydrate beef flavored TVP with warm water. For the chili recipe, cook the vegetables in water. Place all of the veggies, diced, in a saucepan with the spices except for the TVP and beans. Bring to a boil after water. Simmer for 10 minutes.

Add the beans and the rehydrated TVP. Cook for another 10 minutes, then remove the pot from the heat and let it cool. Next, spread a non-stick sheet on dehydrator tray and process at 145 degrees for 8 hours.

Tofu with vegetable bouillon

Ingredients

- *Tofu; 9 oz.*
- *Vegetable bouillon; 6 to 10 g*

Method

In a pan, combine 8 ounces of water with 6 to 10 grams of vegetable bouillon and lightly bring to a boil. Cut noodles or squares of tofu and add in the pan once the bouillon has dissolved.

After simmering the tofu for 10 minutes, turn off the burner till it the bouillon is absorbed. Until the majority or all of the liquid has been absorbed, keep tofu covered in pan. Allow it to cool.

Place a parchment sheet on the dehydrator tray and pour. Dehydrate them at 135 degrees for 8 hours.

Tofu and taco seasoning

Ingredients

- *Chili mix powder; 1 tsp*
- *Cumin; 1 tsp*
- *Salt; ½ tsp*
- *Garlic powder; ¼ tsp*
- *Onion powder; ¼ tsp*
- *Red pepper flakes; ¼ tsp*
- *Oregano; ¼ tsp*
- *Paprika; ¼ tsp*
- *Black pepper; ¼ tsp*
- *Tomato paste; 1 tbs*

Method

In a pan, mix each ingredient with 8 ounces (236 ml) of water and lightly boil some water. Cut tofu in noodles or in cubes and add the seasonings. Let them dissolved. After simmering the tofu for 10 minutes, turn off the burner. Allow them to absorb and cover with a lid.

Place a parchment sheet on the dehydrator tray and pour. Dehydrate them at 135 degrees for 8 hours.

Dried Cauliflower Tots

Ingredients

- *Olive oil; 1 tbs*
- *Yellow onions; ½ minced*
- *Cauliflower riced; 12 oz.*
- *Salt*
- *Ground black pepper; ¼ tsp*
- *Vegetable stock; ½ cup*
- *Garbanzo bean flour; ¼ cup*
- *Nutritional yeast; 2 tbs*
- *Vegan mozzarella ½ cup, shredded*
- *Cooking oil spray*

Method

Add the oil to a medium saucepan on a medium flame. When the pan is shimmering, add the onion and cook for 5 to 6 minutes, add rice-cauliflower and allow to simmer for 5 minutes or till the pieces are soft but not browned. Add pepper, salt and vegetable stock and bring to a boil. Mix the nutritional yeast and chickpea flour in another bowl stirring constantly.

Next add the chickpea flour mixture in the pot, stir, and cook for approximately 7 to 10 minutes and then turn the heat down to low, add the cheese, and simmer the mixture gently while stirring constantly.

Turn of the heat and allow it to cool. Then line dehydrator tray with the silicon mesh or non-stick sheet and pour the batter on to it. dehydrate at 145 degrees for 8 hours.

If you want to eat at home, serve it with beet ketchup.

Dill pickle chickpea crunchies

Ingredients

Basic brine

- Water; ½ cup
- White vinegar; ½ cup
- Apple cider vinegar; ¼ cup
- Light agave nectar; 2 to 3 tsp
- Cooked chickpea; 3 cups

For Seasoning

- Olive oil; 2 tbs
- Roughly chopped fresh dill; ¼ cup
- Garlic cloves; 3, minced
- Kosher salt; 1 tsp
- Mustard powder; ½ tsp
- Ground coriander; ¼ tsp
- Celery seed; ¼ tsp
- Black pepper; 1/8
- Red pepper flake

Method

Shake up the chickpeas and the rest of the brine ingredients in a medium-sized jar and put it in the refrigerator for 12 to 24 hours to marinate. You can marinate it for more time too as the chickpea soak more, the taste will be even better.

Drain the chickpeas completely but don't rinse them. Add the oil in a bowl and chickpeas toss everything together. Make sure they all are coated properly. Spread them on the dehydrator tray lined with the parchment paper in a single layer.

Dehydrate at 140 degrees until they are crisp.

Tofu and curry seasonings

Ingredients

- *Curry powder; 1 tsp*
- *Vegetable bouillon; 1 tsp*
- *Salt; ½ tsp*
- *Black pepper; ¼ tsp*
- *Red pepper flakes; ¼ tsp*
- *Cumin; ¼ tsp*
- *Paprika; ¼ tsp*
- *Turmeric; ¼ tsp*
- *Onion powder; ¼ tsp*
- *Ground ginger ¼ tsp*
- *Cinnamon; ¼ tsp*

Method

In a pan, mix each ingredient with 8 ounces of water and lightly boil some water. Cut tofu in noodles or in cubes and add the seasonings. Let them dissolved. After simmering the tofu for 10 minutes, turn off the burner. Allow them to absorb and cover with a lid.

Place a parchment sheet on the dehydrator tray and pour. Dehydrate them at 135 degrees for 8 hours.

Tofu tortillas

Ingredients

- *Dried taco spiced tofu squares; ½ cup*
- *Tortilla; 2 of 8 inches*

Method

Place the dry tofu cut in squares in the water-filled saucepan. Bring to a boil, then cover with a lid and place in an insulating cozy for at least 15 minutes. Fill tortillas with the rehydrated tofu, then fold them in half.

Matcha munch candied popcorn

Ingredients

- *Freshly popped popcorns; 6 cups*
- *Pepitas; 1 cup*
- *Granulated sugar; ¾ cup*
- *Matcha powder; 2 tsp*
- *Brown rice syrup; ¼ cup*
- *Vegan butter or coconut oil; 1 tbs*
- *Salt; ¼ tsp*
- *Vanilla extract; ½ tsp*
- *Melted chocolate; 4 oz.*

Method

In a pan with the high slide, add oil, matcha, rice syrup, melted butter or coconut oil, sugar, and salt. Whisk the matcha firmly to prevent and remove any tiny clumps. Place the pan on the stovetop and turn the heat to medium. You can also beat the mixture if there are lumps. Keep stirring and when boiled properly, stop whisking and bring it to bubble for 5 minutes.

Remove from heat and add vanilla and pour hot sugar. Make sure they are coated properly. Spread them on the dehydrator tray and dry them for 4 to 6 hours at 135 degrees. This can be stored for 3 to 4 days.

Drizzle the melted chocolate if serving immediately at home.

Tofu vegetable soup

Ingredients

- *Dried rice; ½ cup*
- *Dried tofu; ¼ cup*
- *Dried spring onion; ¼ cup*
- *Dried mushroom; ¼ cup*
- *Vegetable bouillon powder; 1 tsp*
- *Dried vegetable medley; ¼ cup*

Method

Combine all the ingredients in a pot with water and let them sit for 5 minutes. Bring them to a boil and transfer in an insulating cozy for 15 minutes.

Vegetable rice with tofu noodles

Ingredients

- *Dried rice; ½ cup*
- *Dried tofu; ¼ cup*
- *Dried spring onion; ¼ cup*
- *Dried mushroom; ¼ cup*
- *Vegetable bouillon powder; 1 tsp*
- *Dried vegetable medley; ¼ cup*

Method

Combine all the ingredients in a pot with water and let them sit for 5 minutes. Bring them to a boil and transfer in an insulating cozy for 15 minutes.

Curry rice and vegetable TVP

Ingredients

- *Curry-seasoned dehydrated rice; ¾ cup*
- *Chicken flavor TVP; 1/3 cup*
- *Mixed vegetables; 1/3 cup*
- *Water to rehydrate; 2 cups*

Method

Mix all the ingredients dehydrated ingredients in water and let them soak for 5 minutes. Bring them to a boil for a minute and simmer them on a low temperature. Transfer in an insulating cozy and allow them to sit for 15 minutes.

Garlic pita chips

Ingredients

- *Medium pitas; 6*
- *Olive oil; 3 tbs*
- *Garlic cloves; 6 to 8*
- *Dried thyme; 1 tsp*
- *Salt; ¼ to ¾*

Method

Cut the pita bread with bread into thin slices or more like chips. In a bowl, add all the ingredients and whisk them. toss in the pita chips and coat with the mixture.

Place them on the dehydrator tray lined with parchment sheet. Process at 145 degrees for 8 to 10 hours.

Dried Sriracha kettle corn

Ingredients

- *Coconut oil; 3 tbs*
- *Dried Popcorn kernels; ½ cup*
- *Granulated sugar; 1/3 cup*
- *Sriracha; 3 to 5 tsp*
- *Flaky sea salt; ½ to 1 tsp*

Method

Mix salt, sugar, and sriracha in a bowl. On trial take the dehydrated corn kernels and put them in a pan with coconut oil. To test if the heat level is a right, put 2 to 3 kernels first and shake them properly. If they pop, continue to add the remaining kernels with the mixture and keep shaking the pan.

Dehydrating Whole Grain

Ingredient

- *Whole grain berries; 6 cups*

Method

Put the whole grain berries in a crockpot and water. Cook them till they become tender or you can cook them like brown rice. In case you are cooking them like brown rice, add 6 cups of grains with enough water and bring them to a boil. turn down the heat and simmer for about 40 minutes or till the water dries. When done, remove from heat and allow to cool.

Spread on the dehydrator tray lined with a sheet and dehydrate for 115 degrees for 12 to 15 hours.

Dehydrating zoodles and squashes

Ingredients

- *Zoodles and squashes*

Method

Wash and peel it. cut in spiral cutter to make it like spaghetti looking. Place them on the dehydrator rack and let it dry for 8 to 10 hours at 115 degrees.

Curry tofu and vegetables

Ingredients

- *Dried curry seasoned tofu squares or noodles; ½ cup*
- *Dried carrots; ¼ cup*
- *Broccoli, dried; ¼ cup*
- *Dried apples; ¼ cup*
- *Water; 1 ¼ cups*

Method

Place all of the dried ingredients in a saucepan with the water, excluding the milk or coconut milk powder. Bring to a boil, then cover with a cozy to keep warm for fifteen minutes. While there is still some liquid, stir in the milk powder. Wait another five or more minutes.

Carrot wrap

Ingredients

- *Carrot pulp; 2 cups*
- *Water; 2 cups*
- *Flax meal; 1 cup*
- *Curry powder; 1 ¼ tsp*
- *Honey; 1 tsp*
- *Coconut amino; 1 tsp*
- *Garlic powder; ¼ tsp*
- *Kosher salt; ¼ tsp*
- *Cayenne powder; 1/8 tsp*

Method

Blend all the ingredients in a food processor and make them smooth. Pour it on the dehydrator tray lined with a parchment paper and form circles by leaving some space in between. It must be spread in a thin layer.

Let the batter dehydrate for 4 to 6 hours or till they look like wraps. Flip them halfway to ensure that they are dried properly. Be careful so that there must not crack.

Corn silk spice

Ingredients

- *Silk from 16 corn cobs*

Method

To make the silk from the corn cobs, remove all the leaves and husk from its surrounding. Separate the corn cob from the bundle of silk and set it aside. Cut the brown top from the bundles and place them on the dehydrator tray. Spread them evenly in a single layer.

Dry them at 110 for 24 hours or till they are dried completely. When done, let it cool and transfer in a food processor. Blend till they become smooth.

Veggie tofu Scramble

Ingredients

- Olive oil; 1 tbs
- White onion; ½ small
- Carrot; 1, peeled
- Zucchini, small 1
- Garlic; 1 clove
- Super- firm; ½ lb.
- Nutritional yeast; 3 tbs
- Braggs liquid amino; 1 tbs
- Soy sauce; 1 tbs
- Dried parsley; 1 tsp
- Salt; ½ tsp
- Baby spinach; 2 cups

Method

In a pan, pour oil and saute garlic and onion. Cook them for 4 to 5 minutes and stir occasionally. Add carrots, zucchini, and mushroom. Saute for another five minutes. Drain the water and cut tofu in ¾ inch thick cubes. toss them in with the other vegetables and squeeze it with the sides of the pan to turn them in crumbs. Add the remaining seasonings and cook till the liquids are dried. Turn off the flame and allow it to cool. When done, place them on the dehydrator tray and dry for 10 hours at 145 degrees.

Stuffed zucchini bites

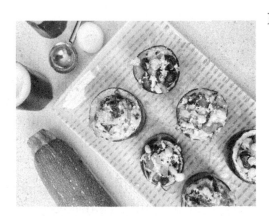

Ingredients

- Zucchini; 4 medium
- Olive oil; 5 tbs
- Large red onion; ½
- Garlic, clove; minced; 2
- Parsley, dried; 1 tsp
- Ground cumin; ¼ tsp
- Dried thyme
- Chopped nuts; 1 cup
- Cannellini beans; 2/3 cup

- Almond meal; ½ cup
- Soy sauce; 1 tbs
- Salt and pepper

Method

Grate zucchini and put it aside. In a pan, heat oil, saute onions till they are translucent and then add garlic, parsley, thyme and the grated zucchini. Cook till they are brown. When done, remove from heat and allow it to cool then transfer in the food processor. Add almond meal, salt, pepper, and soy sauce. Blend roughly and pour in a bowl.

Line the dehydrator tray with the parchment sheet and with the help of a spoon scoop the batter on it. dehydrate at 135 for 5 to 6 hours.

Taco Bite

Ingredients

- *Vegan beef crumble; 1 pack of 12 oz.*
- *black beans; ½ cup*
- *tomato paste; 2 tbs*
- *garlic clove; 1*
- *yellow cornmeal/ ¼ cup*
- *chili powder; ½ tsp*
- *smoked paprika; 1 tsp*
- *cumin, ground; 1 tsp*
- *dried oregano; 1/4 tsp*
- *aquafaba; ½ cup*
- *cilantro; 1/3 cup minced*
- *salt; ½ tsp*
- *crushed tortilla chips; ½ cup*

Method

Place beans, tomato paste, garlic, cornmeal, chili powder, paprika, cumin, oregano, and red pepper flakes, add the meatless crumbles to the food processor. Don't over-blend; just pulse enough to integrate and have slightly crumble the crumbs. Add the salt, cilantro, and aquafaba, pulse the mixture again. Make the meaty dough after blending.

Scoop out balls about the size of walnuts, and then fully cover the outsides of each one with the crumbled tortilla chips and placing them on the parchment sheet of the dehydrator tray. Dehydrate them for 12 to 14 hours at 135 degrees.

Veggie scramble

Ingredients

- *Olive oil; 1 tbs*
- *Small onion; ½ diced*
- *Garlic clove; 1*
- *Peeled carrot; 1*
- *Zucchini; small; 1*
- *Mushroom; 3 diced*
- *Firm tofu; ½ lb.*
- *Nutritional yeast; 3 tbs*
- *Braggs liquid amino; 1 tbs*
- *Soy sauce; 1 tbs*
- *Dried parsley; 1 tbs*
- *Salt; ½ tsp*
- *Baby spinach; 2 cups*

Method

In a pan heat the oil, saute onion, garlic and cook till onion turns translucent. It will take 4 to 5 minutes then add zucchini, mushroom, and carrot. Cook again for 5 minutes till they become tender.

Drain water from tofu and cut it in small cubes. toss them in the pan and then press against the sides of the make them crumbled. Stir and mix them gently and sprinkle the seasonings and mix again. Cook for a minute or two and remove from heat. Allow it to cool.

When done, spread on the dehydrator tray lined with a non-stick sheet. Dehydrate for 6 to 7 hours at 135 degrees.

Loaded baked potatoes with tofu crouton

Ingredients

For Tofu crouton

- *olive oil; 2 tbs*
- *soy sauce; 2 tbs*
- *rice vinegar; 1 tbs*
- *salt*
- *black pepper*
- *extra-firm tofu, drained; 14 oz. 1*

for Potatoes

- *baking potatoes, 4*
- *olive oil; ¼ cup*
- *unsweetened soy milk; 1 to 3 tbs*
- *salt*
- *sweet paprika*
- *scallion; 2*
- *broccoli steamed, chopped; 1 cup*
- *chopped roasted pepper; ½ cup*

Method

In a bowl, add soy sauce, vinegar, salt, oil, and pepper and stir them. cut tofu in small cubes and marinate with the mixture. Allow it to marinate for 1 to 2 hours. wash, peel the potatoes and boil them. when done, mash them with the other vegetables and add the remaining ingredients. Mix them till they are incorporated thoroughly.

Line 2 dehydrator trays with parchment sheet. Place tofu one and Spread thin layer of potato mixtures on the tray. Process for 8 hours at 145 degrees.

When making it at home, instead of boiling, bake the potatoes with a slit and pour the tofu mixture in the middle. Bake them again at 350 degrees for 35 to 40 minutes.

Mahallo Macadamia quinoa pilaf

Ingredients

- *Water; 2 1/3 cup*
- *Hibiscus blossom tea bags; 6 dried*
- *Coconut fat milk; 1 can of 14 oz.*
- *Salt; ½ tsp*
- *Beet puree; ½ cup*
- *Raw quinoa; 2 cups*
- *Macadamia nuts; 1 cup*
- *Coconut oil; 1 tbs*
- *Sweet onion; 1*
- *Garlic cloves; 4*
- *Ground black pepper; ¼ tsp*
- *Scallion; 1 large and thinly sliced*

Method

Bring hibiscus blossom tea to a boil in a pot and remove from heat afterward. Allow the tea to steep for 30 minutes, then squeeze out the tea bags. Take the pot back to heat and add coconut milk, beet puree, salt. Bring them to a boil again and add quinoa next. Turn the heat low allowing it to simmer by covering it. cook them for 20 minutes or till the quinoa absorbs the liquids then turn off the heat.

Roast the macadamia nuts separately in a skillet and set aside. Heat oil and saute the remaining ingredients. Mix them with the nuts and cooked quinoa. Stir till they are incorporated.

Allow them to cool and spread the on the dehydrator tray with parchment sheet. Dry them at 145 degrees for 8 hours.

Dried Texan pinto beans

Ingredients

- *Dry pinto beans; 1 lb.*
- *Vegan bacon; 5 to 6 oz.*
- *Yellow onion; 1 medium*
- *Garlic cloves; 4 minced*
- *Pickled jalapeno; ¼ cup*
- *Chili powder; 2 tbs*
- *Ground cumin; 1 tsp*
- *Salt; tsp*
- *Water; 5 ½ cups*

Method

In a cookpot or pressure cooker, combine all the ingredients and cook on a medium heat. Cooke till it becomes stew. This can take around 15 to 30 minutes. In case it is not done after the mentioned time, make sure it turns stew or in soup, whatever you like. When done, allow it to cool and then spread it on the dehydrator tray.

Process at 135 degrees for 10 to 12 hours.

Dried Tofu poke

Ingredients

- *Tofu; pack, cut in small bite-size cubes*
- *Tomatoes, diced; 1*
- *Ogo limu; chopped; ¼ cup*
- *Scallion, 1 to 2 chopped*
- *Low-sodium soy sauce; ¼ cup*
- *Sesame oil; 1 tbs*
- *Toasted sesame; 2 tsp*
- *Fresh ginger; 1 tsp*
- *Crushed red pepper flakes*

Method

Toss the tofu in oil first and set them aside. In the bowl, cook all the other ingredients by adding them one and add tofu. Mix them well and put them in a sealable bag and marinate overnight. when done, line a non-stick sheet on the dehydrator tray and put the marinated tofu on it.

Process for 10 hours at 135 degrees.

Dried Tofu manicotti

Ingredients

- *Yellow onion; diced; ½*
- *Olive oil; 1 tbs*
- *Minced garlic; 1 ½ tbs*
- *Red wine; ½ cup*
- *Tomatoes, diced; 14 oz. 1 can*
- *Italian seasoning; 2 tbs*
- *Nutritional yeast; 2 tbs*
- *Salt and pepper*
- *Tofu; 1 lb.*
- *Lemon juice; 2 tbs*
- *Granulated sugar; 1 tsp*
- *Salt; 1 tsp*
- *Olive oil; 2 tbs*
- *Italian seasoning; 2 tbs*
- *Vegetable stock; ½ cup*

Method

Make sauce by saute onion and garlic sauce first and then add red wine. Simmer for 2 to 3 minutes and then add tomatoes. Continue simmering for 10 to 15 minutes. Next, add the seasonings and stir thoroughly. When done, turn off the flame and allow to cool.

Cut tofu in ¾ inch cubes and put them aside. In a food processor, combine all the reaming ingredients till they are incorporated. Take a sealable bag and combine all the ingredients and marinate it for 4 to 5 hours. drain the extra marinate and place them on the dehydrator tray lined with a parchment sheet.

Process at 145 degrees for 8 to 10 hours. flip halfway.

Dehydrating Tofu ricotta-stuffed Delicata

Ingredients

- *tofu; 10 oz.*
- *non-dairy milk; ¼ cup unsweetened; ¼ cup*
- *nutritional yeast; ¼ cup*
- *olive oil; 1 tbs*
- *rice vinegar; 1 tbs*
- *fresh lemon juice; 1 tbs*
- *soy sauce; 2 tbs*
- *garlic powder; ½ tsp*
- *onion powder; ½ tsp*

Vegetable and topping

- *Diced cremini/ button mushroom; ½ cup*
- *Frozen spinach; ½ cup*
- *Fresh parsley; ¼ cup*
- *Pine nuts; ¼ cup*

Method

Set the oven to 400 degrees and line a baking dish with aluminum foil. Put aside. Trim the edges and scrape the seeds from squash in half either lengthwise or widthwise. Place them in the baking dish with some space in between.

Process the tofu, non-dairy milk, nutritional yeast, oil, vinegar, lemon juice, soy sauce, garlic, and onion powder in your food processor to turn them into smooth mixture. Add mushrooms, parsley, spinach along with the nuts and combine them. pour it on the layered squash and bake for 45 minutes. When done, allow to cool.

Place them on the dehydrator tray lined with the parchment paper. Cut them baked squash in small and thin squares and put them on the tray. Dehydrate at 145 degrees for 10 hours till they are dried properly.

Dried Thai coconut slider

Ingredient

- *Olive oil; 2 tbs*
- *Diced shallot; ½ cup*
- *Garlic cloves; 2, minced*
- *Red curry paste; 2 tbs*
- *Vegan fish sauce/ soy sauce; 1 tbs*
- *Lime juice; 1 tbs*
- *Dried coconut pulp; 1 cup*
- *Jasmine rice, cooked; 1 cup*
- *Tapioca flour; 2 tbs*
- *Salt and pepper*

Method

Heat oil in the pan and saute shallot with garlic. Pour in curry paste and cook for 2 to 3 minutes, add sauce afterward. Cook them and then transfer to bowl. mix all the other ingredients with them so they are incorporated properly. Add salt and pepper to taste, mix again.

Line a non-stick sheet on the dehydrator tray. Pour and spread a thin layer of the mixture on the tray. Dehydrate it at 145 degrees for 10 hours.

Dehydrated capsicum

Ingredients

- *Capsicum*

Method

Wash, cut the stem and remove the seeds from the capsicum. Cut them into long strips not thicker than ½ inch. Place them on the dehydrator tray and process it for 10 to 12 hours at 120 degrees or till they dry properly.

Sriracha Chickpeas

Ingredients

- *Chickpeas can; 1 of 19 oz.*
- *Salt; 1 tsp*
- *Sugar; 1 tbs*
- *Sriracha; 3 tb*

Method

Wash, drain, and let the chickpeas dry with a kitchen towel. Pat dry them. In a large bowl, add sriracha and salt, mix them well and coat the chickpeas with this mixture. Sprinkle sugar on the top and place them on the dehydrator sheet placed on the dehydrator tray.

Process it at 130 degrees for 10 to 12 hours.

Breadcrumbs dehydrated

Ingredients

- *Bread slices*

Method

Dehydrating breadcrumbs is easy. You need to take the old bread and place them on the dehydrator tray and process it at 125 degrees for 4 hours. This time is not fixed, you need to process them till they become crispy.

When dried properly, process them in the food processors to turn them into crumbs.

Dried Winter Squash

Ingredients

- *Winter Squash*

Method

Cut the squash into slices and remove the seeds and rind. Place them on a dehydrator tray and dry them for 10 to 12 hours at 125 degrees.

Dehydrating Mashed potatoes

Ingredients

- *Potatoes; 1 to 3 lbs.*

Method

Wash potatoes and boil them in salted water till they become soft. It is recommended to over-cook them so the mashing process is smooth. When done, peel and mash them ensuring there are no lumps left. Add seasonings if you want and mix them again.

Place parchment paper and spread the mashed potatoes in an evenly thin layer and process it on a dehydrator tray at 135 degrees for 8 to 10 hours.

Drying Stinging Nettle

Ingredients

- *Drying Stinging Nettle*

Method

Wash and pat dry stinging nettle. Separate their leaves from the stems and place them on the dehydrator tray.

Dry them at 95 degrees for 12 to 18 hours.

Conclusion

Like all good things, we need to come to an end, and with that, we'll conclude our discussion on the dehydration of food for preppers. We hope you now have a better understanding of the basics of dehydration, as well as some tips and tricks for getting the most out of your dehydrator. With this little guide, you can now start creating delicious, healthy, and long-lasting snacks and meals that you can enjoy for months or even years.

As with any activity, safety should always be a priority. From selecting the right ingredients and equipment to proper rehydrating and storage techniques, these tips will ensure your food remains safe and delicious.

Finally, we hope you've gained an appreciation for the art of dehydration. Whether you want to extend the shelf life of your food or simply enjoy tasty snacks, dehydration is a great way to achieve both. So don't be afraid to experiment and have fun with it!

Thank You

Just wanted to let you know how much you mean to me.

Without your help and attention, I couldn't keep making helpful publications like this one.

Once again, I appreciate you reading this book. I absolutely enjoyed writing it, and I hope you did too.

Before you leave, I need you to do me a favor.

Please consider posting a book review for this one on the platform.

Reviews will be used to help my writing.

Your feedback is extremely helpful to me and will help me to generate more. upcoming books in the information genre.

I would love to hear from you.

Gillian.

References

Ahuja, A. (2020, June 2). *All About "Sun Drying" Food: Meaning, Benefits And How It Works*. NDTV Food. https://food.ndtv.com/food-drinks/all-about-sun-drying-meaning-benefits-and-how-it-works-2239586

Boxell, H. (2021). *The Basics Of Food Dehydration: A Complete Guide To Dehydrating Food*. Amazon Digital Services LLC - KDP Print US.

Cancler, C. (2020). *Complete Dehydrator Cookbook: How to Dehydrate Fruit, Vegetables, Meat & More*. Rockridge Press.

Dehydrating Food: Is It Good for You? (2020, January 11). WebMD. https://www.webmd.com/diet/dehydrating-food-good-for-you

Henry, J. (2022). *Dehydrator Cookbook for Preppers: 1200 Days of Easy and Affordable Homemade Recipes to Dehydrate Fruit, Meat, Vegetables, Bread, Herbs. An Essential Guide to Be Totally Prepared for Any Emergency*. Independently published.

How to Dehydrate Foods. (n.d.). MU Extension. https://extension.missouri.edu/publications/gh1563

National Center for Home Food Preservation | How Do I? Dry. (n.d.). Retrieved January 10, 2023, from, https://nchfp.uga.edu/how/dry/pack_store.html

Yadav, A. K., & Singh, S. V. (2012). Osmotic dehydration of fruits and vegetables: a review. *Journal of Food Science and Technology, 51*(9), 1654–1673. https://doi.org/10.1007/s13197-012-0659-2

Porter, B. (2019, May 29). *9 Benefits of Dehydrating Food that May Surprise You*. The Seasonal Homestead. Retrieved January 10, 2023, from, https://www.theseasonalhomestead.com/9-benefits-of-dehydrating-food-that-may-surprise-you/

Silva. (2022, April 22). *Dried and Delicious: The Health Benefits of Dehydrated Foods*. Silva International. Retrieved January 10, 2023, from, https://silva-intl.com/blog/dried-and-delicious-the-health-benefits-of-dehydrated-foods

Times of India. (2018, March 13). *Sure, water can help in Weight loss but so can dehydration! Here's the science - Times of India.* The Times of India. Retrieved January 10, 2023, from https://timesofindia.indiatimes.com/life-style/health-fitness/weight-loss/sure-water-can-help-in-weight-loss-but-so-can-dehydration-heres-the-science/articleshow/63266724.cms

Made in United States
North Haven, CT
15 March 2023